Featured in the cover photo:
Shades o' Green Salad 33
Tomato Aspic 52
Salad-Filled Pineapple Shells 12

The Salad Book

$Culinary\ Arts\ Institute$®

A DIVISION OF DELAIR PUBLISHING COMPANY, INC.

ISBN: 0-8326-0628-6

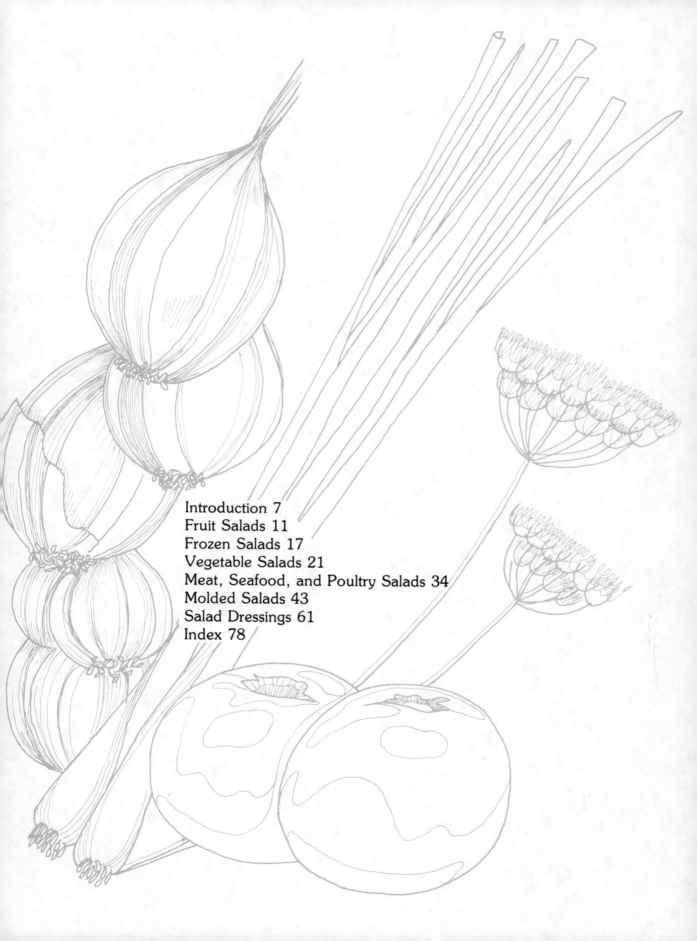

Introduction

Salads and Salad Dressings.

One of the wonderful things about salads is that there are so many of them! Among the exuberant abundance of green salads, vegetable salads, main-dish salads, and molded and frozen salads, there is a favorite for everyone.

For Dad, who fancies himself as a sort of specialty chef, there's the tossed salad which all men enjoy and which only he (so he fondly believes) can mix to perfection. For Mom, who entertains her bridge club every fourth Thursday and is always on the lookout for fabulous new recipes, there's the superlatively delicious frozen salad which is *so* rich—but so good that nobody cares. For Sister, who is sensitive about a tendency to plumpness, there are vegetable salads bursting with vitamins but reassuringly low in calories. And for the youngsters, there are salads which may be arranged to look intriguingly like something else (flowers, faces or animals), and which, served without a dressing, appeal to young tastes and lead them on to a genuine liking for more sophisticated salads.

Salads are family fare because they are packed with the foods everyone needs every day, made attractive by their crispness, their refreshing flavor, and their eye-appeal. Salads are party fare, too, because they are so beautiful, so flavorful, so satisfying—and so easy to serve. Salads come in many forms: they may be appetizers, garnitures, accompaniments, main dishes, desserts, or a whole meal; they may be made individually, or may be big enough to serve the whole party; and they may be crisp and cool, molded, frozen, or even hot!

With all this variety, don't let yourself and your family get into a salad rut!

Salad Pointers

Have all salad ingredients, bowls, and plates thoroughly chilled. With the exception of a very few hot salads, coldness is essential to the appeal of all salads.

Trim and rinse greens under cold running water, handling them carefully to avoid bruising. Shake off the excess moisture and then gently pat them *dry* before putting them into a plastic bag or the vegetable drawer, and into your refrigerator. Wet greens not only make watery salads; they present a surface to which an oil dressing cannot cling.

Allow ample time for chilling. Fine restaurants chill greens and other salad ingredients twenty-four hours before serving salad.

Greens should always be broken or torn, never cut (except in the case of head lettuce which is to be served in wedges or quarters).

Tomatoes may be peeled or not, as your family prefers, for use in salads. Unpeeled tomato shells or tomato cups are sturdier and keep their shape better; peeled ones are easier to cut with a salad fork.

Tomatoes cut in wedges or chunks are delicious additions to many tossed salads, but their juice tends to make the dressing watery unless they are added at the last moment before serving.

Fruits that tend to discolor after peeling or paring (such as avocado, banana, apples, fresh peaches and pears) should be brushed with pineapple or citrus fruit juice unless they are to be tossed immediately with an acid fruit or salad dressing.

The final assembling of ingredients for a salad of fresh fruits, vegetables or greens should be done *just* before serving. Many main-dish salads, potato and macaroni salads, and cooked-vegetable salads improve in flavor when the mixture is prepared an hour or so ahead of serving time and allowed to stand in the refrigerator to chill and blend the individual flavors. But even these mixtures should be combined with their green garnishes at the last moment.

Avoid unnecessary handling of salad materials. Salads should always have that fresh-from-the-refrigerator look which is so appealing to the eye and tempting to the taste. Arrange the fruits or vegetables on the salad plate if the salad requires it, but don't destroy that carefree look by *re*arranging them.

Salad Accompaniments

Salads can be made still more tempting by serving them with appealing accompaniments. Often these are crisp and crunchy: **Melba toast, rye wafers, breadsticks** or **cheese pastry straws.** (Vary Melba toast by brushing it lightly with **butter** in which you have delicately browned **sesame seeds;** or butter the toast and sprinkle with **poppy seeds,** which need no toasting). Another flavorful variation of Melba toast is made by brushing thin slices of **"icebox" rye bread** with **garlic butter** and oven-toasting them until crisp and slightly browned.

Dainty alternatives to the crisp accompaniments are **finger sandwiches** with an assortment of fillings: **water cress** or **cucumber** with **butter, cream cheese** with chopped **nuts** or **olives** (or both), **peanut butter,** or **jelly. Celery Whirls** (page 22) are a pleasing accompaniment which becomes part of the salad.

It's Smart To Be Careful

There's No Substitute for Accuracy

Read recipe carefully.

Assemble all ingredients and utensils.

Select pans of proper kind and size. Measure inside, from rim to rim.

Use standard measuring cups and spoons. Use measuring cups with subdivisions marked on sides for liquids. Use graduated nested measuring cups for dry or solid ingredients.

Check liquid measurements at eye level.

Level dry or solid measurements with straight-edged knife or spatula.

Sift (before measuring) regular all-purpose flour, or not, in accord with the miller's directions on the package. When using the instant type all-purpose flour, follow package directions and recipes. Level flour in cup with straight-edged knife or spatula. Spoon, without sifting, whole-grain types of flours into measuring cup.

For These Recipes—What to Use

Brown Sugar—when substituting brown for granulated sugar, granulated brown sugar may be used; check table on package before pouring sugar into measuring cup.

Cream—light, table or coffee cream containing 18% to 20% butterfat.

Heavy or Whipping Cream—containing not less than 30% butterfat.

Croutons—slices or cubes of toasted bread, plain or browned in melted butter.

Flour—regular all-purpose flour.

Grated Peel—whole citrus fruit peel finely grated through colored part only.

Herbs and Spices—ground unless recipe specifies otherwise.

Oil—salad or cooking type. Use olive oil only when recipe so directs.

Peppercorns—the dried berries of the pepper plant; use ground (in pepper grinder) or whole.

Rotary Beater—hand operated (Dover-type) beater, or use electric mixer.

Stuffed Olives—pimiento-stuffed olives.

Sugar—granulated (cane or beet).

How to Do It

Blanch Almonds—the flavor and crisp texture of almonds are best maintained when almonds are allowed to remain in water the shortest possible time during blanching. Therefore, blanch only about ½ cup at a time; repeat process as many times as necessary for larger amounts. Bring to a rapid boil enough water to cover the shelled almonds. Drop almonds into water. Turn off heat and allow almonds to remain in water about 1 min.; drain or remove with slotted spoon or fork. Place between folds of absorbent paper; pat dry. Squeeze almonds between thumb and fingers to remove skins. Place on dry, absorbent paper; to dry thoroughly, shift frequently to dry spots on paper.

Toast Nuts—place nuts in a shallow baking pan. Heat nuts (plain or brushed lightly with cooking oil) in oven at 350°F until delicately browned. Move and turn occasionally with fork. Or put nuts into a heavy skillet in which butter or margarine (about 1 tablespoon per cup of nuts) has been melted; or use oil. Heat until nuts are lightly browned, moving and turning constantly with a spoon, over moderate heat. If necessary, drain nuts on absorbent paper.

Salt Nuts—toast nuts; sprinkle with salt.

Boil—cook in liquid in which bubbles rise continually and break on the surface. Boiling temperature of water at sea level is 212°F.

Cook Macaroni—Heat to boiling in a large saucepan 3 qts. water and 1 tablespoon salt. Add gradually 2 cups (8-oz. pkg.) uncooked macaroni (elbows, shells or tubes broken into 1-in. pieces). Boil rapidly, uncovered, 10 to 15 min., or until tender. Test tenderness by pressing a piece against side of pan with fork or spoon.

Drain macaroni by turning it into a colander or large sieve; rinse with hot water to remove loose starch.

Cut Dried Fruits (uncooked) or Marshmallows—use scissors dipped frequently in water.

Dice—cut into small cubes.

Flake Fish—with a fork, separate canned or cooked fish into flakes (layer-like pieces). Remove bony tissue from crab meat; salmon bones are edible.

Fold—use flexible spatula. Slip it down side of bowl to bottom. Turn bowl quarter turn. Lift spatula through mixture along side of bowl with blade parallel to surface. Turn spatula over so as to fold lifted material across the surface. Cut down and under again; turn bowl and repeat process until material is blended to desired degree. With every fourth stroke, bring spatula up through center.

Grind Cooked Meat—trim meat from bone. Remove any excess fat. Put meat through medium blade of food chopper.

Hard-Cook Eggs—put eggs into large saucepan and cover completely with cold or warm water. Cover pan. Bring water rapidly just to boiling. Turn off heat immediately; if necessary to prevent further boiling, remove pan from heat source. Let eggs stand, covered 20 to 22 min. Plunge eggs into cold, running water. Crackle shells under water and roll between hands to loosen shells. When cooled, start peeling at large end.

Note: Eggs are a protein food and therefore should never be boiled.

Marinate—allow food to stand in liquid (usually an oil and acid mixture) to impart additional flavor.

Mince—cut or chop into small, fine pieces.

Panbroil Bacon—place in a cold skillet only as many bacon slices as will lie flat. Cook slowly, turning frequently. Pour off fat as it collects. When bacon is evenly crisped and browned, remove from skillet and drain on absorbent paper.

Prepare Quick Broth—dissolve in 1 cup hot water, 1 chicken bouillon cube for chicken broth or 1 beef bouillon cube (or ½ teaspoon concentrated meat extract) for meat broth.

Rice—force through ricer, sieve or food mill.

Sieve—force through sieve or food mill.

Simmer—cook in a liquid just below boiling point, in which bubbles form slowly and break below the surface.

Vegetable Preparation

Clean Celery—Trim off root end and cut off leaves. (If desired, leaves may be left on inner stalks when they are to be served as a relish. Cut-off leaves may be chopped and used to give added flavor to soups and stuffings.) Separate stalks, remove blemishes and wash.

Clean Garlic—Separate into cloves and remove thin, papery outer skin. Prepare as directed in recipe.

Clean Green or Red Pepper—Rinse and slice away from pod and stem; trim off any white membrane; rinse away seeds; cut into strips; dice or prepare as directed in recipe.

Clean Onions (dry)—Cut off root end and a thin slice from stem end; peel and rinse. Prepare as directed in recipe.

Clean Radishes—Wash firm radishes. Cut off root and stem ends. Prepare as directed in recipe.

Peel Tomatoes—Rinse; dip into boiling water to loosen skins. Peel and chill in refrigerator. Cut out stem ends and prepare as in recipe.

When Using the Electric Blender
To grind, put enough food in blender container at one time to cover blades; cover, turn on motor and grind until very fine. (Turning motor off and on helps to throw food back on blades.) Empty container and grind next batch of food.

Fruit Salads

Fruit Preparation

Apples, Pears—Wash fruit. Cut into quarters, remove core and, if desired, pare and cut into lengthwise slices. Toss fruit with pineapple or citrus fruit juice to help prevent discoloration.

Avocados—Rinse avocados, peel, cut into halves lengthwise and remove pits. Brush surfaces with lemon juice to help prevent discoloration.

Bananas—Peel bananas having brown-flecked peel and cut into crosswise slices. Toss slices gently with pineapple or citrus fruit juice to help prevent discoloration.

Blueberries, Raspberries—Sort and rinse berries; drain thoroughly.

Cherries—Sort, rinse and drain cherries. Remove stems, cut into halves and remove pits.

Grapes—Rinse and drain grapes thoroughly. Cut large bunches into small clusters.

Melons—Rinse melons and cut into halves. With a knife or spoon, remove seedy center.

For Melon Balls—Using melon-ball cutter, carefully cut balls.

For Melon Bowls—Rinse melons and cut into halves. If a scalloped edge is desired using a narrow sharp-pointed knife, carefully carve around each melon half. If a saw-toothed edge is desired, do not cut melons into halves. Using a narrow sharp-pointed knife, mark points in a saw-tooth line at 1-in. intervals around center of melon. Cut on line between points marked and pull halves apart. With a knife or spoon, remove seedy center from melon halves. Using a spoon or melon-ball cutter, scoop out meat from melon halves keeping surface smooth and leaving shells about ½ in. thick. Chill shells and pieces in refrigerator.

For Melon Rings—Rinse melon and cut into halves, crosswise. With a knife or spoon, remove seedy center. Cut melon into ¾-in. slices, reserving ends. With a sharp paring knife, remove the rind from each ring. Using a melon-ball cutter, carefully cut balls from inside of melon ends. Meat removed from the ends may be used in other food preparation. Chill melon rings and balls in refrigerator.

Nectarines—Rinse nectarines, cut into halves and remove pits.

Oranges, Grapefruit—Rinse fruit. With a sharp knife, cut away peel and white membrane from fruit. Remove sections by cutting on either side of the dividing membranes; remove, section by section, over a bowl to collect juice. Discard seeds, if any.

For Grapefruit Baskets—Rinse grapefruit and cut into halves. With a grapefruit knife or a sharp paring knife, loosen each section by cutting down and along either side of dividing membranes. Cut completely around outer skin to loosen membrane from shell. Remove grapefruit sections and reserve for use in

food preparation. Remove and discard membrane and fibrous center. To make a handle for basket, about ¼-in. down from top of each half-shell carefully cut through peel and around shell, leaving a 1-in. piece attached at opposite sides of the shell. Bring the strips up together at the center and secure with a small piece of thread or short piece of wooden pick. Decorate center of handle with a sprig of water cress or mint, or a small flower.

Peaches—Rinse peaches; plunge into boiling water to loosen skins. Immediately plunge into cold water; gently slip off skins. Cut peaches into halves; remove pits. Brush cut surfaces with lemon juice to prevent discoloration.

Pineapple—Cut off and discard crown (spiny top) and rinse pineapple. Cut into crosswise slices. With a sharp knife, cut away and discard rind and "eyes" from each slice. Cut away the core and cut the rings into wedges.

For Pineapple Shells—Rinse pineapple. To prepare, cut whole pineapple into halves lengthwise through crown (spiny top). Cut out and discard core. With a grapefruit knife or sharp paring knife, carefully remove and reserve fruit from pineapple halves, leaving shells about ½ in. thick. Cut reserved pineapple into pieces and chill in refrigerator with the pineapple shells.

Strawberries—Sort, rinse, and drain berries. Remove hull or leave on for garnish.

Fruit Plates

Arrange chilled **fresh** or **canned fruit** attractively on a chilled plate lined with cool crisp **salad greens.** Top with a scoop of **Cranberry Sherbet** (page 16) or other sherbet. Garnish the plate with **Cream Cheese-Nut Balls** or **Frosted Grapes** if desired.

For Cream Cheese-Nut Balls—Prepare chopped **pecans** or chopped toasted **almonds.** Beat 3 oz. (1 pkg.) **cream cheese** until softened. Form cream cheese into balls and roll in chopped nuts.

For Frosted Grapes—Beat 1 **egg white** until frothy. Dip small clusters of rinsed, thoroughly drained **grapes** into beaten egg white. Shake off excess, then dip grapes into **sugar.** Set aside to dry. Chill grapes in refrigerator if desired.

Citrus-Avocado Salad—Have fruit chilled before preparing the salad. Place bowl of chilled **salad dressing** in center of a large chilled salad plate. Line the plate with crisp **salad greens.** Arrange **grapefruit sections** and **avocado slices** alternately around the bowl. Cut **oranges** (peel removed) crosswise into slices. Arrange slices, overlapping in a circle around the grapefruit and avocado. Garnish with **berries** or **pomegranate seeds.**

Fruit-Filled Melon Rings—Prepare **Melon Rings** Fill with available **fresh fruit;** use fruit that harmonizes in color with the melon rings. If desired, sprinkle fruit with **lemon** or **lime juice** or with any desired **liqueur** (creme de menthe, kirsch, Cointreau or Curacao). Garnish with **mint sprigs.** Serve with **Orange Fruit-Salad Dressing** (page 71), **Pineapple Salad Dressing** (page 70), **Enchanting Fruit Dressing I or II** (page 73).

Fresh Pear Luncheon Salad—Line a chilled serving platter with crisp **lettuce** and **water cress.** Arrange chilled **fresh Anjou pear halves,** cut side up, on one side of the platter. Arrange strips of **cheese** and/or cold cooked **chicken** or **turkey, luncheon meat, ham** or **roast meat** on the opposite side of the platter. Garnish with **Celery Whirls** (page 22). If desired, serve with **French Dressing.**

Salad-Filled Pineapple Shells—Prepare **Pineapple Shells.** Shells may be filled with chilled available **fresh fruit, Chicken Salad** (page 40, mix in some of the fresh pineapple pieces, if desired) or a **sea food salad.** For a dessert salad, mix chilled **fruit** with a small amount of **Syrup for Fruit;** spoon mixture into pineapple shells. Top fruit with a small scoop of **sherbet.** Garnish the stem end of each pineapple shell with a thin half slice of **lime.** Garnish with **mint sprigs.**

For Syrup for Fruit—Mix 1 cup **sugar** and 1 cup **water** together in a saucepan. Stir over low heat until sugar is dissolved. Cover, bring to boiling and boil 5 min. Cool. Stir in about 1 tablespoon **lime juice** or 1 teaspoon **vanilla extract.** Store in refrigerator and use as needed. When sweetening fruit, for a special flavor accent, use **Vanilla Confectioners' Sugar.**

For Vanilla Confectioners' Sugar—Set out a 1- to 2-qt. container having a tight-fitting cover. Fill with **confectioners' sugar.** Remove a **vanilla bean,** about 9 in. long, from its air-tight tube, wipe with a damp, clean cloth and dry. Cut vanilla bean into quarters lenghtwise; cut quarters crosswise into thirds. Poke pieces of vanilla bean down into the sugar at irregular intervals. Cover container tightly and store.

Note: Tightly covered sugar may be stored for several months; add more sugar when necessary. Replace vanilla bean when aroma is gone.

Waldorf Salad

2   **medium-size red apples (about 2 cups, diced)**
1   **cup chopped celery**
½   **cup (about 2 oz.) chopped walnuts**
¼   **teaspoon salt**
¼   **cup mayonnaise**

1. Wash apples, quarter, core and dice.
2. Combine with celery and walnuts.
3. Sprinkle with salt.
4. Add mayonnaise and toss lightly.
5. Chill in refrigerator until ready to serve.
6. Serve in crisp lettuce cups (page 21). If desired, sprinkle with paprika or cinnamon.
About 4 servings.

Empress Salad

Escarole
Watermelon chunks
Pear cubes (unpared)
Cucumber cubes (pared)
French Dressing (page 64; use lemon juice)

1. Wash and thoroughly chill salad ingredients before preparing salad. Set out a salad bowl.
2. Tear escarole into pieces.
3. Prepare watermelon chunks, pear cubes, and cucumber cubes.
4. Put the fruit and cucumber cubes into the salad bowl with the escarole. Pour on French dressing (using just enough to coat fruit and greens).
5. Toss lightly and serve immediately.

Stuffed Avocados

Avocado halves form colorful and delicious bases for many different salad mixtures. First brush their cut surfaces with fresh **lemon** or **lime juice** to prevent discoloration. Then heap them with fresh **citrus-fruit salad, drizzling French dressing** over it; or with **shrimp, lobster, crab meat** or **sea food salad;** or with **chicken** or **turkey salad.** For buffet service, arrange the filled avocado halves on a bed of crushed ice (tinted if desired) in a crystal bowl.

Overnight Coconut Fruit Salad

1   **11-oz. can mandarin oranges (about 1 cup, drained)**
1   **8¼-oz. can crushed pineapple (about ¾ cup, drained)**
1   **cup orange sections**
8   **(2 oz.) marshmallows**
1   **cup (about 4 oz.) moist shredded coconut, cut**
1   **cup thick sour cream**
2   **tablespoons sugar**

1. Drain, reserving syrup for use in other food preparation, contents of can of mandarin oranges and can of crushed pineapple.
2. Prepare and section enough oranges to yield 1 cup orange sections.
3. Cut marshmallows into quarters.
4. Put the mandarin oranges, pineapple, orange sections and marshmallows into a large bowl with the moist shredded coconut.
5. Mix together sour cream and sugar.
6. Pour over the fruit mixture and toss lightly to mix thoroughly. Cover; chill in refrigerator overnight.
7. To serve, spoon portions of salad onto chilled serving plates lined with crisp salad greens. Garnish with mint sprigs.

About 6 servings

White Fruit Salad

Orange or Apricot Fruit-Salad Dressing (one-half recipe, page 71)
1   **20-oz. can pineapple chunks (about 2 cups, drained)**
1   **17-oz. can pitted light sweet cherries (about 1¼ cups, drained)**
3   **medium-size (about 1 lb.) apples**
¾   **cup (about 4 oz.) blanched, toasted almonds**
16   **(¼ lb.) marshmallows**
2   **bananas with brown-flecked peel**
2   **teaspoons lemon juice**

1. Prepare and chill orange or apricot fruit-salad dressing.
2. Drain cans of pineapple and cherries thoroughly, reserving pineapple syrup (cherry syrup may be saved for use in other food preparation).
3. Put drained fruit into a bowl and set in refrigerator to chill.
4. Wash apples, quarter, core, pare and cut into small pieces.
5. Put apple pieces into a small bowl and pour over them ½ cup of the reserved pineapple syrup. Set in refrigerator to chill thoroughly (2 to 3 hrs.)
6. Meanwhile, coarsely chop almonds and set aside.
7. Shortly before serving, cut marshmallows into quarters.
8. Peel banana and score (by drawing tines of a fork lengthwise over entire banana), and cut crosswise into ¼-in. slices.
9. Put banana into a large bowl and drizzle with lemon juice.
10. Toss lightly to coat banana slices evenly with the lemon juice.
11. Remove chilled fruit from the refrigerator. Thoroughly drain the apple pieces; add to the bowl of banana slices with the pineapple chunks, cherries, almonds and marshmallows.
12. Spoon over the fruit as much chilled dressing as desired. Toss lightly to mix thoroughly.
13. When ready to serve, arrange curly endive on chilled salad plates and carefully spoon a portion of the fruit salad onto each serving plate. If desired, garnish with mint sprigs.

6 to 8 servings

Overnight Fruit Salad: Follow recipe for White Fruit Salad. Prepare **Dressing for Overnight Fruit Salad** (page 61). Use only pineapple chunks, light sweet cherries and marshmallows, increasing marshmallows to 24 (6 oz.) Prepare and section 4 medium-size **oranges**. Slice ½ cup **maraschino cherries** and set aside on absorbent paper to drain. Add the marshmallow, oranges and maraschino cherries to the bowl with the fruit. Spoon the dressing over the fruit mixture and toss lightly. Cover; chill in refrigerator overnight.

Sour Cream Fruit Salad: Follow recipe for White Fruit Salad or recipe for Overnight Fruit Salad; omit the dressing. Add 1 cup **thick sour cream** to the fruit mixture and toss lightly.

Sherbets for Fruit Salads

Creamy Lemon Sherbet

1¼   **cups sugar**
½   **cup lemon juice**
2   **teaspoons grated lemon peel**
⅛   **teaspoon salt**
2   **cups cream**
    Few drops yellow food coloring

1. Set refrigerator control at colder operating temperature. Set a bowl and rotary beater in refrigerator to chill.
2. Blend together sugar, lemon juice, lemon peel, salt, cream and yellow food coloring in a bowl, in order.
3. Stir until sugar is dissolved. Pour into refrigerator tray and set in freezing compartment of refrigerator. Freeze until mixture is mushlike in consistency.
4. When mixture is mushlike, turn out into the chilled bowl and beat with the chilled beater until smooth. Immediately return mixture to refrigerator tray and freeze until firm.

1½ pts. sherbet

Creamy Lime Sherbet: Follow recipe for Creamy Lemon Sherbet. Substitute **lime juice** and grated **lime peel** for the lemon juice and lemon peel. Substitute **green food coloring** for yellow food coloring.

Creamy Tangerine Sherbet: Follow recipe for Creamy Lemon Sherbet. Use only 2 tablespoons lemon juice. Add to it ½ cup **tangerine juice.** Substitute 2 teaspoons grated **tangerine peel** for lemon peel. Substitute 2 to 3 drops **orange food coloring** for yellow food coloring.

Grapefruit Sherbet: Follow recipe for Creamy Lemon Sherbet. Decrease sugar to ½ cup. Substitute 1¼ cups **grapefruit juice** for lemon juice and 2 teaspoons grated **grapefruit peel** for lemon peel. Decrease cream to 1¾ cups. Substitute 2 drops **red food coloring** for yellow food coloring.

Creamy Orange Sherbet: Follow recipe for Creamy Lemon Sherbet. Use only 2 tablespoons lemon juice. Add to it ½ cup **orange juice.** Omit lemon peel. Substitute **orange food coloring** for yellow food coloring.

Cranberry Sherbet

4 cups (about 1 lb.) cranberries
2 cups boiling water
¾ lb. marshmallows (about
  48)
1 cup orange juice
¼ cup sugar
2 tablespoons lemon juice
1 teaspoon grated orange
  peel

1. Set refrigerator control at colder operating temperature. Set a large bowl and a rotary beater in refrigerator to chill.
2. Wash, sort, and put cranberries into a saucepan.
3. Add water.
4. Cover and cook over medium heat until cranberry skins burst (about 10 min.).
5. Meanwhile, set out marshmallows.
6. Cut into quarters and put in top of double boiler with orange juice.
7. Heat over simmering water until marshmallows are melted but still fluffy, stirring occasionally. Remove from heat and set aside.
8. When cranberry skins have all burst, force cranberries and liquid through a food mill or sieve. Immediately add sugar and lemon juice to the hot sieved berries, stirring until sugar is dissolved.
9. Add marshmallow mixture to cranberry mixture, together with orange peel.
10. Blend well and turn into refrigerator trays. Set in freezing compartment of refrigerator and freeze until mixture is mushlike in consistency.
11. When mixture is mushlike, turn out into the chilled bowl and beat with the chilled beater just until smooth (not until melted). Return mixture to refrigerator tray and freeze until firm.

About 1 qt. sherbet

Fruit Salad with Ice Cream Topping

4 pears, cored
1 large melon wedge
1 can Mandarin Orange
  Wedges
½ can pineapple
  green grapes (optional)
2 pints vanilla ice cream
1 cup fresh orange juice
  orange rind

1. Cut the pears and melon wedge in pieces and mix with the canned fruits.
2. Pour in a little of the syrup from the cans. Cover and let salad stand in refrigerator until chilled.
3. Divide the ice cream into 8 dishes.
4. Distribute fruit on top of ice cream.
5. Just before serving, pour on the fresh orange juice. Sprinkle with finely slivered orange rind or coconut.

Serves 8

Marinated Fruit Salad

2 apples
3 pears
3 peaches
1 pineapple
  confectioners sugar
¼ cup rum or Cointreau

1. Pare, core and slice apples and pears. Halve, pit, peel and slice peaches. Cut pineapple into chunks.
2. Place fruit in a bowl and sprinkle with confectioners sugar to taste. Sprinkle with rum or Cointreau.
3. Cover the bowl tightly and chill for at least 6 hours so the sugar draws out fruit juices.

Serves 8

Frozen Salads

Frozen Fruit Salad

½ cup (about 3 oz.) almonds
1 20-oz. can crushed pineapple (about 1¾ cups, drained)
½ cup maraschino cherries
½ cup (about 3 oz.) pitted dates
24 (6 oz.) marshmallows
8 oz. cream cheese, softened
¼ cup mayonnaise
1 cup chilled whipping cream

1. Set refrigerator control at colder operating temperature. Set a bowl and rotary beater in refrigerator to chill. Set out a 1½-qt. mold or large refrigerator tray.
2. Blanch, toast, and salt almonds.
3. Chop coarsely and set aside.
4. Set out can of crushed pineapple to drain, reserving syrup.
5. Cut maraschino cherries into quarters and set aside on absorbent paper to drain. (To avoid a pink tint in the mixture, drain cherries thoroughly.)
6. Cut dates into slivers and set aside.
7. Cut marshmallows into eighths and set aside.
8. Beat until well blended 3 tablespoons of the reserved pineapple syrup and cream cheese.
9. Mix in mayonnaise.
10. Gently mix in nuts, fruits and marshmallows.
11. Using the chilled bowl and beater, beat chilled whipping cream until cream is of medium consistency.
12. Lightly spread over cheese mixture and fold together. Turn into mold or refrigerator tray. Freeze until firm (about 4 hrs.),
13. Unmold onto chilled serving plate and garnish base with **fruit** and sprigs of **mint** or **water cress**. Or serve slices or wedges of the salad on chilled individual salad plates.
14. Serve with **pineapple salad dressing** (page 70).

8 to 10 servings

Frozen Tropical Salad: Follow recipe for Frozen Fruit Salad. Substitute **pecans** for almonds and ¾ cup diced **banana** for the dates.

Note: If desired, turn salad mixture into 2 29-oz. cans or 3 16-oz. cans, washed and drained. Freeze until firm.

Frozen Fruit Salad Delicious

⅓ cup (about 1½ oz.) walnuts

3 tablespoons finely chopped maraschino cherries

1 8¼-oz. can crushed pineapple (about ¾ cup, drained)

2 cups thick sour cream

¾ cup sugar

2 tablespoons lemon juice

⅛ teaspoon salt

1 medium-size banana having brown-flecked peel

1. Set refrigerator control at colder operating temperature. Line 10 2½-in. muffin-pan wells with paper baking cups.
2. Coarsely chop walnuts and set aside.
3. Set aside maraschino cherries on absorbent paper to drain. (To avoid a pink tint in the mixture, drain cherries thoroughly.)
4. Drain can of crushed pineapple reserving syrup for use in other food preparation.
5. Mix together sour cream, sugar, lemon juice and salt.
6. Blend in the pineapple, walnuts and cherries.
7. Peel and dice banana.
8. Mix in the diced banana. Spoon mixture into the baking cups; put into freezing compartment of refrigerator and freeze until firm.
9. Before serving, remove paper cups. Allow salads to stand at room temperature for a few minutes to soften very slightly.

10 servings

Pear and Frozen Cheese Salad

4 oz. Roquefort or Blue cheese (about 1 cup, crumbled)

½ cup chopped celery

3 oz. (1 pkg.) cream cheese, softened

¼ cup mayonnaise

1 tablespoon lemon juice

¼ teaspoon salt

⅛ teaspoon pepper

½ cup chilled whipping cream

4 chilled ripe Bartlett pears
lemon juice
curly endive, water cress, or other salad greens

1. *For Frozen Roquefort or Blue Cheese Cubes*—Set refrigerator control at colder operating temperature. Set a bowl and rotary beater in refrigerator to chill.
2. Crumble Roquefort or blue cheese into a bowl.
3. Set aside.
4. Prepare celery and set aside.
5. Beat cream cheese until fluffy.
6. Mix in mayonnaise, lemon juice, salt and pepper, stirring until thoroughly blended after each addition.
7. Stir in the crumble cheese and chopped celery. Set mixture aside.
8. Using the chilled bowl and beater, beat cream until it is of medium consistency (piles softly).
9. Gently fold into cheese mixture. Turn into a refrigerator tray. Put into freezing compartment of refrigerator and freeze until firm.
10. When ready to serve, cut frozen cheese mixture into 1-in. cubes.
11. *For Bartlett Pear Salad*—Rinse pears, cut into halves and core.
12. Brush cut sides of pears with lemon juice.
13. Place curly endive, water cress, or other salad greens on each of 8 chilled salad plates.
14. Put one pear half, cut side up, on each plate. Place two or three frozen Roquefort or Blue Cheese Cubes in hollow of each pear half. Or arrange greens, pear halves and cheese cubes on a large chilled serving plate.
15. Serve immediately with **French dressing.**

8 servings

Pear-Cabbage-Cheese Cube Salad: Follow recipe for Frozen Roquefort or Blue Cheese Cubes. Add 1½ cups chopped **cabbage** with crumbled cheese and celery, and mix well. Substitute 1/8 teaspoon **paprika** for the pepper. Increase whipping cream to 1 cup. Complete as in recipe.

Greengage Plum Salad

2½	cups canned greengage plums and syrup (about 2¼ cups, sieved)
1	cup chopped celery
½	cup (about 2 oz.) chopped walnuts

1. Set refrigerator control at colder operating temperature.
2. Cut plums into halves, remove and discard pits, and force plums and syrup through a sieve or food mill.
3. Prepare and mix in celery and walnuts.
4. Turn into a refrigerator tray.
5. Put into freezing compartment of refrigerator and freeze until mixture is firm (about 4 hrs.), stirring 2 or 3 times.

6 to 8 servings

Frozen Peppermint Dessert Salad

1	20-oz. can crushed pineapple (about 2½ cups)
1	3-oz. pkg. strawberry-flavored gelatin
1	pkg. (10½ oz.) miniature marshmallows
¼	cup (about 2 oz.) cinnamon candies
2	cups chilled whipping cream
¼	lb. soft butter mints, crushed

1. Put pineapple, gelatin and marshmallows into a large bowl.
2. Add cinnamon candies.
3. Mix well, cover and put into refrigerator to chill overnight.
4. Meanwhile, set refrigerator control at colder operating temperature. Set a bowl and rotary beater in refrigerator to chill.
5. Using the chilled bowl and beater, beat whipping cream (one cup at a time) until cream is of medium consistency (piles softly).
6. Fold whipped cream into pineapple mixture with butter mints.
7. Turn into refrigerator trays or a 10-in. tubed pan. Freeze until firm.

About 20 servings

Note: The strawberry-flavored gelatin is used for flavor and color rather than for gelling the mixture.

Nippy Cheese Freeze Salad

10	stuffed olives
3	oz. natural cheese food
½	cup thick sour cream
1	teaspoon lemon juice
3	drops Tabasco
	Lettuce
	Curly endive
	Romaine
	Water cress
1	clove garlic, cut into halves

1. *For Nippy Cheese Freeze* — Set refrigerator control at colder operating temperature.
2. Chop olives and set aside.
3. Put cheese food into a small bowl and mash with a fork.
4. Add sour cream gradually, blending until mixture is smooth.
5. Blend in the chopped olives, lemon juice and Tabasco.
6. Turn mixture into a 1-qt. refrigerator tray. Put into freezing compartment of refrigerator and freeze until mixture is firm.
7. *For Tossed Salad* — Rinse, lettuce, curly endive, romaine and water cress discarding bruised leaves, drain and dry thoroughly.
8. Using as much of each green as desired, tear into pieces enough greens to yield about 2 qts. Put into a large plastic bag or vegetable freshener. Chill in refrigerator at least 1 hr.
9. When ready to serve, rub a salad bowl with cut surface of garlic.
10. Cut the frozen cheese mixture into small cubes.
11. Put the chilled greens into the salad bowl and toss lightly with **French dressing.** Add the cheese cubes and toss just enough to distribute the cubes evenly throughout the greens.
12. Serve immediately.

6 to 8 servings

Garlic Cottage-Cheese Freeze: Follow recipe for Nippy Cheese Freeze Salad. Use two refrigerator trays. Substitute **ripe olives** for stuffed olives and 2 cups sieved **cream-style cottage cheese** for cheese food. Blend in 1 clove **garlic** crushed in garlic press or minced.

Cucumber Frost

16 (¼ lb.) marshmallows
2 medium-size (about 1½ lbs.) cucumbers
⅓ cup lemon juice
½ to 1 teaspoon grated onion
½ teaspoon salt
Few grains cayenne pepper
Green food coloring (about 3 drops)
2 egg whites
1 tablespoon sugar
6 Tomato Shells (page 23)
Lettuce leaves

1. Set refrigerator control at colder operating temperature. Set a bowl in refrigerator to chill.
2. *For Cucumber Frost (About 1 qt.)* — Cut marshmallows into quarters and put into the top of a double boiler.
3. Place over simmering water, stirring occasionally until softened.
4. Meanwhile, rinse and pare cucumbers.
5. Cut into halves lengthwise; remove and discard seeds. Grate enough of the cucumbers to yield 2 cups pulp and juice. Drain pulp; mix lemon juice, onion, salt and cayenne pepper with the juice.
6. Add green food coloring gradually to the marshmallows, stirring over simmering water until mixture is completely blended and smooth. Add the cucumber pulp and blend well. Tint by blending in, a drop at a time.
7. Pour mixture into refrigerator tray and freeze until mushlike in consistency.
8. When mixture is mushlike, beat egg whites until frothy.
9. Add sugar and beat until rounded peaks are formed.
10. Turn the cucumber mixture into the chilled bowl and beat with rotary beater just until smooth. Add the egg white mixture and fold in thoroughly.
11. Return mixture to refrigerator tray and freeze until firm (3 to 4 hrs.).
12. *To Complete Salad* — Prepare and chill tomato shells.
13. When ready to serve, line chilled salad plates with lettuce leaves.
14. Put one tomato shell on each plate. Put a scoop of Cucumber Frost in the center of each tomato.

6 servings

Vegetable Salads

Salad Green Varieties and Preparation

The many varieties of greens star in the tossed salad and form the background of other salads. Select greens that are fresh, blemish-free and crisp. In general, wash them before storing, drain thoroughly and gently pat dry with a soft, clean towel or absorbent paper. Place in the refrigerator in the vegetable drawer or a plastic bag, or wrap tightly in aluminum foil or other moisture-vapor-proof material to prevent wilting.

Never soak greens when washing them. If necessary, crisp them by placing for a short time in ice and water. Before using, remove all moisture left from washing or crisping.

Lettuce—Discard bruised and wilted leaves; rinse, drain and dry. (For *Lettuce Cups*, remove the core from head lettuce with a sharp, pointed knife; let cold water run into the core cavity to loosen the leaves; drain thoroughly; gently pull leaves from head; cut off heavy, coarse ends; pat dry.) The following are types of lettuce: *Head or Iceberg*—firm, compact head with medium-green outside leaves, pale-green heart. *Butterhead or Boston*—loose, lighter-weight head with light-green outside leaves, light-yellow heart; less crisp than Iceberg. *Romaine or Cos*—elongated green head with coarser leaves having stronger flavor than Iceberg. *Bibb or Limestone*—head similar in size and shape to Boston; deep-green leaves with delicate flavor. *Leaf*—leafy bunches of curly-edged leaves; many varieties are grown commercially and in the home garden. A bright attractive touch for lettuce is achieved by dipping the curly edges of leaves in a paste made of two parts of paprika and one part of water.

Cabbage—Store in a cool place without washing. Discard bruised and wilted outside leaves, rinse, cut into quarters and remove core; chop or shred as directed in the recipe. The following are varieties of cabbage: *Early or new*—pointed heads with light-green leaves. *Danish-type*—staple winter cabbage; compact head heaving pale-green or white leaves. *Savoy*—round head of yellowish, crimped leaves. *Celery or Chinese*—long, looser head of pale-green to white leaves.

Endive—Discard bruised and wilted leaves; rinse; drain; dry. The following are varieties of endive: *Curly endive (often called chicory)*—bunchy head with narrow, ragged-edged curly leaves; dark green outside, pale-yellow heart; pleasantly bitter flavor. *Escarole—(broad-leaf endive)*—bunchy head of broad leaves that do not curl at tips; dark-green outer leaves, pale-yellow heart; less bitter than curly endive. *French endive (Witloof chicory)*—thin, elongated stalk, usually bleached while growing.

Kale—Curly-leafed member of cabbage family; dark green; leaves may have slightly browned edges as a result of frost in growing season. Trim off tough stems and bruised or wilted leaves; wash; drain; dry.

Parsley—Discard coarse stems and bruised leaves; wash gently but thoroughly in cold water; drain and shake off excess water; pat dry. Store in tightly covered jar or plastic bag in refrigerator.

Spinach—Discard tough stems, roots and bruised or wilted leaves. Wash leaves thoroughly by lifting up and down several times in a large amount of cold water; lift leaves out completely and pour off water; repeat in several changes of water until all sand and grit are removed. Drain; pat dry.

Water cress—See Parsley. Water cress may be stored without washing, if preferred. Let the tied bunch stand in a jar or bowl containing enough cold water to reach about halfway up the stems. Cover and store in refrigerator. When ready to use, snip off the amount needed, rinse, drain and shake off excess water.

Other greens—*Field salad*—spoon-shaped leaves; *finocchio*—anise-flavored stalk (serve like celery); *Swiss chard and beet, dandelion mustard and turnip greens*—use tops only.

Raw Vegetable Relishes

Use raw vegetables for colorful, easy-to-prepare relishes. Select only those that are in prime condition—fresh, crisp, preferably young and tender. Clean them thoroughly; with a sharp knife, trim ends where necessary and cut the vegetables into varied shapes as suggested. Chill before serving.

Carrot Curls—Wash and pare or scrape **carrots.** Cut into halves lengthwise. Using a vegetable parer, shave into paper-thin strips. Curl each around finger and fasten with a wooden pick. Chill thoroughly in ice and water. Drain and remove picks before serving.

Carrot Sticks—Wash and pare or scrape **carrots.** Cut into narrow strips about 3 in. long. Chill in refrigerator. If desired, draw carrot sticks through pitted **ripe or green olives;** place as accents on relish tray or salad plates.

Cauliflowerets—Remove leaves, cut off all the woody base and trim any blemishes from head of **cauliflower.** Separate into flowerets. Let them stand in cold salted water for a few minutes to remove dust or small insects which may have lodged in the cauliflower. Drain, rinse, drain again and chill in refrigerator.

Double Celery Curls—Clean **celery.** Cut into 2½ to 3-in. lengths. Slit into narrow parrallel strips, cutting from each end almost to center. Chill until curled in ice and water. Drain before serving.

Stuffed Celery—Clean celery. Prepare **Roquefort** or **Blue Cheese Stuffer** or **Cheddar Cheese Stuffer** (see Celery Whirls, page 22) and fill stalks. Cut stalks into 2-in. lengths. Chill before serving.

Fluted Cucumber Slices—Draw tines of a fork lengthwise over entire surface of rinsed **cucumbers.** Cut into thin slices.

Green Onions (scallions)—Cut off roots and trim green tops to 2 or 3 in., discarding any wilted or bruised parts. Peel and rinse.

Green Pepper Rings—Rinse whole **green peppers** and cut a thin slice from top of each. Carefully remove all white fiber and seeds; rinse cavity. Drain and cut crosswise into thin slices. For strips, cut peppers into halves lengthwise. Clean; slice lengthwise into strips.

Radish Fans—Clean **red** or **white radishes.** Cut thin, lengthwise, parallel slices, leaving them connected at the base. Chill in ice and water until slices spread apart. Drain.

Radish Roses—Wash firm red **radishes.** Cut off root ends. On each, leave a bit of stem and a fresh leaf or two for garnish. With a sharp knife, cut petal. Chill in ice and water until petals spread apart. Drain before serving.

Tomato Wedges—Rinse firm **tomatoes.** Peel if desired. Cut out stem ends and chill. Cut chilled tomatoes into 6 or 8 wedges.

Vegetable Boats, Bowls and Shells

Cabbage Bowl—Rinse firm **green** or **red cabbage** head. If necessary, level base by cutting a thin slice from core end. Form the bowl by cutting out center of cabbage head. Shred the cabbage removed from the head for cabbage salads or **Shrimp Slaw.** Spoon completed salad into bowl and serve. Cabbage bowls also make attractive containers for other salads.

Cucumber Boats—Rinse (do not pare) firm **cucumbers.** Cut into halves lengthwise. Using a spoon. Scoop out centers. Chill in refrigerator.

Green Pepper Shells—Rinse and cut a thin slice from stem end of **green peppers.** Remove seeds; using edge of spoon, cut away white fiber. Rinse cavities. Invert the shells and set aside to drain. Chill in refrigerator.

Tomato Shells—Rinse firm **tomatoes** and peel if desired. Chill in refrigerator. Cut a slice from top of each tomato. Using a spoon, remove pulp. Invert shells and set aside to drain. Chill and sprinkle lightly with salt before filling.

Celery Whirls

1	**medium-size bunch celery**
4	**oz. Roquefort or Blue cheese (about 1 cup, crumbled)**
3	**oz. (1 pkg.) cream cheese, softened**
1	**tablespoon mayonnaise**
2	**teaspoons lemon juice**
1	**teaspoon onion juice**
¼	**teaspoon garlic salt**
	Few grains cayenne pepper
4	**oz. Cheddar cheese (about 1 cup, grated)**
3	**oz. (1 pkg.) cream cheese, softened**
3	**tablespoons milk or cream**
1½	**teaspoons dry mustard**
½	**teaspoons salt**
	Few grains pepper
	Few drops Tabasco

1. Clean celery.
2. Set aside to drain on absorbent paper while preparing one of the cheese stuffers.
3. *For Roquefort or Blue Cheese Stuffer*—Crumble Roquefort or blue cheese and set aside.
4. Thoroughly blend together 3 oz. cream cheese and mayonnaise.
5. Add crumbled cheese and beat until mixture is thoroughly blended. Blend in lemon juice and onion juice and a mixture of garlic salt and cayenne pepper.
6. Mix thoroughly.
7. *For Cheddar Cheese Stuffer*—Grate cheese and set aside.
8. Thoroughly blend together 3 oz. cream cheese and milk or cream.
9. Add grated cheese and beat until mixture is thoroughly blended. Blend in a mixture of dry mustard, salt and pepper.
10. Stir in few drops of Tabasco.
11. Mix thoroughly.
12. *To Complete Whirls*—Fill full-length crisp stalks of celery with one of the stuffers. Rearrange filled stalks in natural shape of celery bunch. Wrap bunch tightly in waxed paper, moisture-vapor-proof material or aluminum foil, and set in refrigerator to chill for several hours.
13. Cut into crosswise slices ¼ to ½ in. thick.

About 1½ doz. whirls

Gourmet Artichoke Salad

4 medium-size artichokes
1 tablespoon lemon juice

1. With a sharp knife, cutting straight across, trim 1 in. from tops of artichokes.
2. Cut off stems about 1 in. from base and remove outside lower leaves. Trim off with scissors and discard the tips of uncut leaves. Let stand in cold salted water for a few minutes to remove any dust or small insects which may have settled in the artichokes. Rinse in clear water and drain upside down.
3. Cook artichokes uncovered, in boiling salted water to cover, adding lemon juice to water.
4. Cook 25 to 45 min., or until a leaf can be easily pulled from artichoke. (Cooking time will depend upon the size of artichokes.) If more water is needed to keep artichokes covered during cooking, add boiling water.
5. Remove artichokes and drain upside down so that all water can run out. Cut off remainder of the stem. Chill artichokes in refrigerator until ready to serve.
6. Serve the artichokes on individual salad plates with **mayonnaise.** Garnish with **lemon slices.**

4 servings

Note: To eat artichokes, pull out the leaves, dip in mayonnaise and eat one by one by drawing them between the teeth to remove only the tender portion at the base. Discard the less tender portion. If choke is present, cut it out with knife and fork after leaves are eaten and discard it . Cut heart or base into pieces and eat with a fork.

Dramatic Cauliflower Salad

1 medium-size head cauliflower
1½ cups French Dressing (one and one half time recipe, page 64)
2 medium-size ripe avocados
2 teaspoons lemon juice
¼ teaspoon salt
¼ teaspoon nutmeg
⅛ teaspoon pepper
½ cup (about 3 oz.) toasted blanched almonds (page 9)
Crisp lettuce leaves

1. Remove leaves, cut off all the woody base and trim any blemishes from cauliflower.
2. Let stand in cold salted water for a few min. to remove any dust or small insects which settle in the cauliflower. Drain.
3. Cook, uncovered, in a 1-in. depth of boiling salted water for 5 min., then covered for 15 to 20 min., or until tender but still firm. Drain.
4. Put the whole cauliflower into a deep bowl and pour French dressing over it.
5. Set in refrigerator to marinate 1 to 2 hrs., turning several times.
6. Meanwhile, prepare and cut avocados into pieces.
7. Force avocado through a sieve or food mill into a bowl. Blend in lemon juice, salt, nutmeg and pepper.
8. Set in refrigerator to chill.
9. Coarsely chop almonds and set aside.
10. When ready to serve, drain the cauliflower. Arrange on a chilled serving plate crisp lettuce leaves.
11. Place drained cauliflower on lettuce. Spread avocado mixture over cauliflower. Top with the chopped almonds.

About 8 servings

Minted Cucumber Salad

1   **medium-size cucumber**
1   **cup thick sour cream**
1   **teaspoon finely chopped fresh mint leaves or ½ teaspoon crushed dried mint leaves**
1   **clove garlic crushed in a garlic press or minced**
½   **teaspoon salt**
    Few grains white pepper

1. Rinse cucumber (do not pare) and coarsely shred.
2. Mix together sour cream, mint leaves, garlic, salt and white pepper.
3. Blend in the shredded cucumber. Set in refrigerator to chill thoroughly.

4 to 6 servings

Minted Pea Salad: Follow recipe for Minted Cucumber Salad. Substitute 2 cups chilled cooked **peas** for the cucumber.

Cucumbers in Creamy Sweet-Sour Dressing: Follow recipe for Minted Cucumber Salad. Thinly slice cucumber into a bowl. Omit sour cream mixture. Blend together, stirring constantly, ¼ cup **cream,** 1 tablespoon **cider vinegar,** 1 teaspoon **sugar,** ¼ teaspoon **salt** and few grains **pepper.** Pour over cucumber and mix gently. Chill.

Marinated Green Bean Salad

3   **cups cooked green or wax beans**
1⅓   **cups cider vinegar**
⅔   **cup water**
½   **cup sugar**
1   **onion, cut into halves**
1   **tablespoon mixed pickling spices**

1. Put green or wax beans into a bowl.
2. Combine vinegar, water, sugar, onion and pickling spices in a saucepan.
3. Set over direct heat and stir until sugar is dissolved. Bring to boiling. Remove from heat; pour over the green beans. Lightly toss together. Cool. Set in refrigerator to marinate overnight.
4. To serve, drain beans; remove the onion. Put beans into a salad bowl; or serve on lettuce lined individual salad plates. Garnish with thinly sliced **onion rings** and **pimento strips.**

About 6 servings

Green Bean Salad Parmesan: Follow recipe for Marinated Green Bean Salad. Lightly toss ⅓ cup chopped **onion** with beans before serving. Omit onion rings.

Hearty Kidney Bean Salad

1½   **to 2 cups kidney beans, drained**
½   **cup (2 oz.) finely diced Cheddar cheese**
½   **cup chopped sweet pickle**
½   **cup chopped celery**
⅓   **cup chopped onion**
½   **cup salad dressing**
1   **teaspoon cider vinegar**
1   **teaspoon sugar**
1   **teaspoon cream**
¼   **teaspoon salt**
    Few grains pepper

1. Put kidney beans, cheddar cheese, sweet pickle, celery and onion into a bowl and toss lightly.
2. For Dressing—Mix together salad dressing, cider vinegar, sugar, cream, salt and pepper.
3. Turn dressing over salad mixture and toss lightly until vegetables are coated.

4 to 6 servings

Kidney Bean Salad: Follow recipe for Hearty Kidney Bean Salad. Omit cheese, celery and dressing mixture. Toss 4 diced **hard-cooked eggs** and 3 tablespoons **sweet pickle liquid** with bean mixture. Blend in a mixture of ½ cup **salad dressing** and 1 tablespoon **pickle liquid.**

Lima Bean Salad

2	cups cooked lima beans
1	tablespoons chopped pimiento
1	tablespoon chopped chives
2/3	cup thick sour cream
1	tablespoon wine vinegar
2	teaspoons lemon juice
1	teaspoon sugar
3/4	teaspoon salt
1/8	teaspoon white pepper

1. Lightly toss together lima beans, pimiento and chives.
2. Mix together sour cream, wine vinegar, lemon juice and a mixture of sugar, salt and white pepper.
3. Add sour cream mixture to lima beans and toss lightly together until all beans are coated with dressing. Set in refrigerator to chill for at least 1 hr.

About 4 servings

Creamy Cole Slaw

1/2	cup thick sour cream
1/2	cup mayonnaise
1	tablespoon lemon juice
2	teaspoons celery seed
1	teaspoon sugar
1/4	teaspoon salt
	Few grains cayenne pepper
4	cups (about 1 lb.) shredded cabbage

1. Blend together thoroughly sour cream, mayonnaise, lemon juice, celery seed, sugar, salt and cayenne pepper.
2. Set in refrigerator to chill.
3. Prepare cabbage.
4. Put cabbage into a bowl and set in refrigerator to chill.
5. Shortly before serving, remove cabbage from refrigerator and pour over it enough of the chilled dressing to moisten. Toss lightly until cabbage is well coated. Serve immediately.

6 to 8 servings.

Apple Cole Slaw: Follow recipe for Creamy Cole Slaw. Decrease sour cream to 1/4 cup and shredded cabbage to 3 cups (about 3/4 lb.). Substitute **pepper** for cayenne pepper. Just before serving, wash, quarter, core and thinly slice 3 **red apples.** Lightly toss apple slices with the cabbage.

Tangy Cabbage Salad: Follow recipe for Creamy Cole Slaw. Substitute **French dressing** for sour cream. Omit lemon juice and seasonings. Blend in 1 teaspoon **dry mustard,** 1/4 teaspoon **curry powder** and 1/4 teaspoon **salt.** Garnish with **pimiento** and sprigs of **parsley.**

Sunshine Slaw: Follow recipe for Creamy Cole Slaw. Decrease shredded cabbage to 3 cups (about 3/4 lb.). Lightly toss 1 cup shredded **carrot** (about 1/2 lb.) and 1/4 cup fine **green pepper** slivers with the cabbage.

Tart Cabbage Salad: Follow recipe for Creamy Cole Slaw. Decrease shredded cabbage to 3 cups (about 3/4 lb.). Omit mayonnaise sour cream mixture. Mix together 2½ tablespoons **cider vinegar,** 1 teaspoon grated **onion,** 1 tablespoon **sugar,** 1 teaspoon **salt** and 1/8 teaspoon **pepper.** Pour over shredded cabbage and toss lightly.

Cabbage and Peanut Salad

4	cups (about 1 lb.) shredded cabbage
¾	cup mayonnaise
¼	cup sugar
2	tablespoons cider vinegar
	Few grains pepper
1	cup (about 5 oz.) salted Spanish peanuts

1. Prepare shredded cabbage.
2. Put cabbage into a bowl and set in refrigerator to chill .
3. Blend together mayonnaise, sugar, cider vinegar and few grains of pepper and set in refrigerator to chill.
4. Shortly before serving, remove cabbage from refrigerator. Pour the chilled dressing over the cabbage. Toss lightly until cabbage is well coated.
5. Mix in peanuts.
6. Serve immediately.

About 8 servings

Wilted Lettuce

1	medium-size head lettuce
6	slices bacon, diced
½	cup cider vinegar
¼	cup water
3	tablespoons sugar
½	teaspoon salt

1. Rinse lettuce and drain thoroughly.
2. Tear lettuce into pieces. Put into a large bowl and set in refrigerator to chill.
3. Panbroil bacon until crisp, reserving fat.
4. Set aside.
5. Return to skillet ¼ cup of the reserved bacon fat and add vinegar, water, sugar and salt.
6. Heat mixture to boiling, stirring well. Mix in the bacon. Immediately pour vinegar mixture over the lettuce and toss lightly to coat lettuce leaves thoroughly.
7. Serve at once.

About 6 servings

Wilted Cabbage: Follow recipe for Wilted Lettuce. Substitute 4 cups shredded **cabbage** (about 1 lb.) for the lettuce. Stir ¼ teaspoon **dry mustard** into vinegar mixture.

Red Cabbage-Almond Slaw

3	cups (about ¾ lb.) shredded red cabbage
½	cup (about 3 oz.) whole toasted blanched almonds (page 9)
1	13¼-oz. can pineapple tidbits (about 1 cup, drained)
⅓	cup salad dressing

1. Put cabbage into a bowl and chill in refrigerator.
2. Prepare almonds and set aside.
3. Thoroughly drain pineapple bits, reserving syrup.
4. Blend together and chill 1 tablespoon reserved pineapple syrup and salad dressing.
5. Shortly before serving, mix cabbage lightly with almonds and pineapple. Spoon dressing over cabbage mixture and toss lightly.

About 6 servings

Red 'n' Green Slaw: Follow recipe for Red Cabbage-Almond Slaw. Decrease red cabbage to 2 cups and add 1 cup shredded **green cabbage.** Omit almonds and pineapple. Blend 2 tablespoons **cream,** 1 tablespoon **tarragon vinegar,** 1 teaspoon prepared **mustard** and ¼ teaspoon **garlic salt** into the salad dressing.

Sour-Cream Potato Salad

6   medium-size (about 2 lbs.) potatoes
½   cup French dressing
3   eggs
1   cup diced cucumber
½   cup chopped celery
⅓   cup finely chopped onion
2   tablespoons chopped chives
2   tablespoons chopped parsley
1   teaspoon salt
½   clove garlic, crushed in a garlic press or minced
1   cup thick sour cream
    Green Pepper Shells (page 23)
    or Cucumber Boats (page 23)

1. Wash potatoes. Cook (see Hot Potato Salad, page 29). Peel potatoes, cut into cubes and put into a bowl with French dressing.
2. Set in refrigerator to marinate for about 2 hrs., turning several times.
3. Meanwhile, hard cook eggs and chill.
4. Coarsely chop the eggs and add to the potatoes together with cucumber, celery, onion, chives, parsley, salt and garlic.
5. Add sour cream.
6. Mix lightly until vegetables are well coated. Set in refrigerator to chill thoroughly before serving.
7. Meanwhile, prepare and chill green pepper shells or cucumber boats.
8. To serve, lightly fill with salad mixture.

6 servings

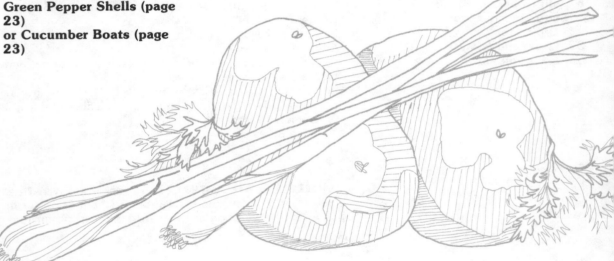

Curried Potato Salad

6   medium-size (about 2 lbs.) potatoes (about 4 cups, cubed)
1   teaspoon salt
1   teaspoon curry powder
3   tablespoons French dressing
2   tablespoons lemon juice
1   teaspoon garlic salt
½   teaspoon salt
¼   teaspoon curry powder
⅛   teaspoon pepper
3   eggs
1   cup diced celery
½   cup diced green pepper
½   cup mayonnaise

1. Wash, pare and cut potatoes into cubes.
2. Cook covered in boiling water to cover, with 1 teaspoon salt and 1 teaspoon curry powder.
3. Cook 8 to 10 min., or until tender when pierced with a fork. Do not overcook. Drain.
4. Dry potatoes by shaking pan over low heat. Put into a bowl with French dressing, lemon juice, garlic salt, ½ teaspoon salt, ¼ teaspoon curry powder and pepper.
5. Set in refrigerator to marinate 1 to 2 hrs., turning several times.
6. Meanwhile, hard-cook eggs and chill.
7. Prepare celery and green pepper.
8. Dice the hard-cooked eggs. Add to the potatoes the diced eggs, celery, green pepper and mayonnaise.
9. Toss lightly to coat all ingredients evenly. Set in refrigerator to chill thoroughly before serving.

About 6 servings

Hot Potato Salad

6	medium-size (about 2 lbs.) potatoes
1	cup (about 2 medium-size) finely chopped onion
3	tablespoons finely chopped parsley
1¼	teaspoons salt
¼	teaspoon pepper
⅔	cup cider vinegar
⅓	cup water
1½	teaspoons sugar
1	egg
⅓	cup salad oil

1. Wash potatoes.
2. Cook covered in boiling salted water to cover 20 to 30 min., or until potatoes are tender when pierced with a fork. Drain. Dry potatoes by shaking pan over low heat. Peel, cut into ¼ in. slices, put into a bowl and add onion, parsley and a mixture of salt and pepper.
3. Toss together lightly and set aside.
4. Mix together vinegar, water and sugar in a small saucepan and heat to boiling.
5. Beat egg slightly.
6. Continue beating while gradually adding the vinegar mixture. Add salad oil gradually, while beating constantly.
7. Pour dressing over potato mixture and toss lightly to coat evenly. Turn salad into a large skillet and set over low heat for 10 to 15 min., or until potatoes are heated. Keep mixture moving gently with a spoon.
8. Serve immediately.

About 6 servings

Brandied Tomatoes I

4	medium-size tomatoes
¼	cup brandy
½	teaspoon salt
⅛	teaspoon pepper
	Chopped parsley

1. Rinse tomatoes, peel and chill.
2. Cut chilled tomatoes into thin vertical slices. Put tomato slices into a shallow dish and cover with a mixture of brandy, salt and pepper.
3. Set in refrigerator to marinate about 2 hrs., carefully turning several times.
4. When ready to serve, arrange tomato slices in a chilled salad bowl. Pour brandy marinade over tomatoes. Garnish with chopped parsley.
5. Serve at once.

About 6 servings

Brandied Tomatoes II: Follow recipe for Brandied Tomatoes I. After marinating, drain and reserve brandy marinade. Put tomato slices into a chilled salad bowl. Mix 1 tablespoon **olive oil** and 1 tablespoon **cider vinegar** with the reserved marinade and pour over tomato slices. Lightly toss together. Garnish with thin **onion rings** and chopped **parsley**..

Cottage Cheese-Filled Tomatoes

6 **Tomato Shells (page 23)**
2 **cups cream-style cottage cheese**
2 **tablespoons salad dressings**
5 **slices crisp panbroiled bacon, crumbled**
2 **tablespoons grated onion**
4 **teaspoons capers**
¼ **teaspoon pepper**

1. Prepare tomato shells.
2. Chill in refrigerator until ready to assemble salad.
3. Thoroughly blend together cottage cheese and salad dressing.
4. Mix in lightly but thoroughly bacon, onion, capers and pepper.
5. Chill in refrigerator.
6. When ready to serve, lightly fill tomato shells with cottage cheese mixture. If desired, garnish with sprigs of **parsley**.

6 servings

Deviled Cottage Cheese Filling: Follow recipe for Cottage Cheese-Filled Tomatoes. Omit bacon and capers. Blend ⅓ cup (3 oz. can) **deviled ham** and ¼ teaspoon **curry powder** with cheese mixture.

Tomato-Caviar Temptation

4 **large tomatoes**
4 **eggs**
12 **rolled anchovy fillets**
2 **tablespoons thick sour cream**
1 **tablespoon salad dressing**
¼ **teaspoon grated onion**
2 **drops Tabasco**
⅛ **teaspoon garlic salt**
⅛ **teaspoon celery salt**
Few grains white pepper
4 **oz. sharp Cheddar cheese (about 1 cup, shredded)**
½ **teaspoon prepared horse-radish**
½ **teaspoon Worcestershire sauce**
2 **drops Tabasco**
¼ **teaspoon salt**
⅛ **teaspoon dry mustard**
⅛ **teaspoon pepper**
¼ **cup thick sour cream**
3 **tablespoons salad dressing**
1½ **cups cream-style cottage cheese**
⅓ **cup finely chopped sweet pickles**
1 **tablespoon salad dressing**
⅛ **teaspoon salt**
⅛ **teaspoon onion salt**
Few grains pepper
8 **slices bacon**
Salad greens (such as lettuce or curly endive)
Thick sour cream
Caviar
French Dressing (page 64)

1. Rinse tomatoes, peel and chill.
2. For Stuffed Eggs—Hard-cook eggs and chill.
3. Set out anchovy fillets.
4. Reserve one egg for the Cheese Spread. Cut the remaining eggs into halves lengthwise. Remove egg yolks to a bowl and mash with a fork or force through ricer or sieve into the bowl. Mix in 2 tablespoons thick sour cream, 1 tablespoon salad dressing, onion and 1 or 2 drops tabasco and a mixture of garlic salt, celery salt and white pepper until thoroughly blended.
5. Lightly fill the egg whites with the egg-yolk mixture. Poke two of the anchovy fillets into each stuffed egg. Chill in refrigerator.
6. For Cheese Spread—Shred cheddar cheese and set aside.
7. Finely chop or sieve the reserved egg into a bowl. Add and mix in the cheese and horse-radish and 1 to 2 drops of tabasco and a mixture of ¼ teaspoon salt, dry mustard and 1/8 teaspoon pepper.
8. Blend in ¼ cup thick sour cream and 3 tablespoons salad dressing.
9. Set in refrigerator to chill thoroughly.
10. For Cottage Cheese Filling—Lightly mix cottage cheese, sweet pickles and 1 tablespoon salad dressing and a mixture of 1/8 teaspoon salt, onion salt and few grains of pepper.
11. Set in refrigerator to chill thoroughly.
12. Dice and panbroil bacon until very crisp.
13. Drain on absorbent paper.
14. Just before serving salad, lightly mix bacon pieces into the cottage cheese mixture.
15. To Complete Salad—Rinse salad greens, drain, pat dry and chill.
16. Arrange on 6 chilled individual salad plates.
17. Cut the chilled tomatoes into 12 slices about ½ in. thick. Place one slice on each salad plate. Spoon Cottage Cheese Filling over slices, allowing about ¼ cup for each slice. Top with re-

maining tomato slices. Spread tomato slices with the Cheese Spread, and place Stuffed Eggs, filling side down, on top.

18. Spoon over eggs a mixture of sour cream and caviar.

19. If desired, top salad with more caviar.

20. Sprinkle French dressing over lettuce leaves around the salad.

21. Serve with **Melba toast** or crusty **hard rolls**.

6 servings

Green Goddess Salad

Green Goddess Salad Dressing (page 69)
Salad greens (such as lettuce, curly endive or escarole)

1. Prepare and chill green goddess salad dressing.
2. Rinse salad greens, discard bruised leaves, drain and dry.
3. Using as much of each green as desired, tear into pieces enough greens to yield about 2 qts. Put into a large plastic bag or vegetable freshener. Chill in refrigerator.
4. When rady to serve, turn salad greens into a chilled bowl. Add the dressing and gently turn and toss until greens are evenly coated.
5. Serve immediately.

6 to 8 servings

Green Goddess Salad with Crab Meat:
Follow recipe for Green Goddess Salad. Drain, remove and discard bony tissue, and separate contents of 2 6½-oz. cans **crab meat** (about 2⅔ cups, drained). Lightly toss crab meat with salad greens.

Green Goddess Salad with Shrimp: Follow
recipe for Green Goddess Salad. Cook 1 lb. **fresh shrimp** with shells (see Cooked Shrimp, page 36). Lightly toss shrimp with salad greens.

Salade Niçoise

Salad Dressing, below
3 medium-sized cooked potatoes, sliced
1 pkg. (9 oz.) frozen green beans, cooked
1 clove garlic, cut in half
1 small head Boston lettuce
2 cans (6½ or 7 oz. each) tuna, drained
1 mild onion, quartered and thinly sliced
2 ripe tomatoes, cut in wedges
2 hard-cooked eggs, quartered
1 can (2 oz.) rolled anchovy fillets, drained
¾ cup pitted ripe olives
1 tablespoon capers

1. Pour enough salad dressing over warm potato slices and cooked beans (in separate bowls) to coat vegetables.
2. Before serving, rub the inside of a large shallow salad bowl with the cut surface of the garlic. Line the bowl or a large serving platter with the lettuce.
3. Unmold the tuna in center of bowl and separate into chunks.
4. Arrange separate mounds of the potatoes, green beans, onion, tomatoes, and hard-cooked eggs in colorful grouping around the tuna. Garnish with anchovies, olives, and capers.
5. Pour dressing over all before serving.

6 to 8 servings

Salad Dressing: Combine in a jar or bottle ½ cup olive oil or salad oil, 2 tablespoons red wine vinegar, a mixture of 1 teaspoon salt, ½ teaspoon pepper, and 1 teaspoon dry mustard, 1 tablespoon finely chopped chives, and 1 tablespoon finely chopped parsley. Shake vigorously to blend well before pouring over salad.

About ⅔ cup

French Endive Salad with Melbourne Dressing

**Melbourne Salad Dressing
(page 68)
Leaves of French endive**

1. Prepare and chill Melbourne salad dressing.
2. Meanwhile, rinse and drain leaves of French endive.
3. Put into a plastic bag and set in refrigerator to chill.
4. Just before serving, arrange leaves of endive on individual salad plates. Shake the dressing well and drizzle over the endive. (Store remaining dressing in a covered container in refrigerator).
5. Serve immediately.

Ceasar Salad

¼   **cup olive oil**
¼   **cup lemon juice**
¼   **teaspoon Worcestershire Sauce**
     Curly endive
     Lettuce
     Romaine
     Water cress
2   **slices toasted bread**
2   **tablespoons olive oil**
3   **cloves garlic, cut in halves**
¾   **cup grated Parmesan cheese**
½   **teaspoon dry mustard**
½   **teaspoon salt**
¼   **teaspoon pepper**
1   **egg**
     Anchovy fillets (about 12 to 15)

1. Chill a large salad bowl.
2. For Dressing—Mix together ¼ cup olive oil, lemon juice and 1 clove garlic.
3. Chill in refrigerator 1 hr.
4. For Salad Greens—Rinse curly endive, lettuce, romaine and water cress, discarding bruised leaves, drain and dry thoroughly.
5. Using as much of each green as desired, tear into pieces enough greens to yield about 2 qts. Put into a large plastic bag or a vegetable freshener. Chill in refrigerator at least 1 hr.
6. When the dressing is chilled, remove and reserve that garlic. Return dressing to refrigerator.
7. For Croutons—Stack and, if desired, trim crusts from bread.
8. Cut bread into ½-in. cubes.
9. Heat 2 tablespoons olive oil over low heat in a large skillet.
10. Add the clove of garlic from the dressing, with an additional clove of garlic, cut in halves.
11. Add bread cubes to the skillet and move and turn gently over medium heat until all sides of the cubes are lightly coated with oil and browned. Remove from heat.
12. To Complete Salad—Rub the salad bowl with cut surfaces of 1 clove garlic, cut in halves.
13. Turn chilled salad greens into the bowl. Sprinkle over greens a mixture of Parmesan cheese, dry mustard, salt and pepper.
14. Shake the chilled salad dressing well and pour it over the greens.
15. Break egg into a small bowl.
16. Add to the seasoned greens. Gently turn and toss salad until greens are coated with dressing and no trace of egg remains. Add the croutons and toss lightly to mix thoroughly. Top with anchovy fillets (about 12 to 15).
17. Serve at once.

6 to 8 servings

Blue Cheese Special: Follow recipe for Caesar Salad. Substitute ½ cup (about 2 oz.) crumbled **Blue cheese** for the Parmesan cheese. Omit dry mustard and anchovy fillets.

Shades o' Green Salad

French Dressing (page 64)
3 oz. (about 3 cups) spinach
4 stalks Pascal celery
½ green pepper
1 cucumber, rinsed
½ head lettuce
2 tablespoons chopped chives
6 green olives
1 small avocado

1. Chill 6 individual salad bowls in refrigerator.
2. Prepare and chill French dressing.
3. Remove and discard tough stems, roots and bruised leaves from spinach.
4. Wash, drain and pat dry. Use part of the spinach to line the salad bowls. Set remainder aside.
5. Cut celery, pepper and cucumber into pieces or slices.
6. Rinse lettuce, drain and pat dry.
7. Tear lettuce and reserved spinach into pieces. Toss vegetables with lettuce, spinach and chives.
8. Add about ⅓ cup of the French dressing; toss lightly to coat greens evenly. (Store remaining dressing in a covered container in refrigerator.)
9. Arrange individual portions of salad in bowls.
10. Pit and slice olives.
11. Rinse, peel, cut into halves lengthwise, remove pit and slice avocado.
12. Garnish salads with avocado and olive slices.

6 servings

Romaine Salad Bowl: Follow recipe for Shades o' Green Salad. Substitute **Tarragon French Dressing** (page 65) for the French Dressing. Substitute 1 head **romaine** for the spinach. Omit olive and avocado garnish.

Green and White Salad Bowl: Follow recipe for Shades o' Green Salad. Substitute **Roquefort French Dressing** (page 65) for the French Dressing. Lightly toss with salad greens 1 cup raw **cauliflowerets** (bite-size), washed and soaked. Omit olive and avocado garnish.

Surprise Green Salad Bowl: Follow recipe for Shades o' Green Salad. Prepare and chill **Roquefort or Blue Cheese Stuffer** (see Celery Whirls, page 22). Stuff **Pascal celery stalks.** Omit olive and avocado garnish. When ready to serve, cut stuffed celery into crosswise pieces and toss lightly with salad greens and dressing.

Chef's Salad Bowl: Follow recipe for Shades o' Green Salad. Substitute a large bowl for individual bowls. Omit chives, olives and avocado. If desired, substitute or add other salad greens such as **curly endive, romaine, Bibb** or **leaf lettuce.** Hard-cook chill and slice 3 **eggs.** Clean and slice enough radishes to yield ½ cup sliced **radishes.** Rinse, peel and chill 2 medium-size **tomatoes.** Cut each tomato into 6 wedges. Cut into thin strips enough cooked chicken and Swiss or Cheddar cheese to yield 1 cup cooked **chicken strips** (see **Stewed Chicken,** (page 40) and 1 cup **cheese strips.** Cut into thin strips enough cooked **ham, tongue, bologna** or **salami** to yield 1 cup. Canned luncheon meat or cooked meats such as **pork, lamb, beef** or **veal** may also be used. When ready to serve, fill the bowl with the salad greens; lightly toss with the prepared vegetables and egg slices. Pour some of the dressing over salad mixture. Toss lightly to coat evenly. Arrange cheese, chicken and meat strips over salad. If desired, garnish with **anchovy fillets.**

Meat, Seafood &
Poultry Salads

Roast Beef Salad

1	**egg**
3	**cups cold roast beef cubes**
¼	**cup quick meat broth (page 9)**
1	**uncooked egg yolk**
1	**tablespoon cider vinegar**
1	**teaspoon dry mustard**
⅓	**cup salad oil**
2	**tablespoons chopped parsley**
1	**tablespoon finely chopped anchovy fillets**
1	**teaspoon capers**
¾	**teaspoon thyme**

1. Hard-cook 1 egg and chill.
2. Cut into cubes enough cold roast beef to yield 3 cups.
3. Drizzle meat broth over beef mixing to coat cubes.
4. Set in refrigerator to chill.
5. Cut the hard-cooked egg into halves. Chop the egg white and set aside.
6. For Dressing—Mash the egg yolk with a fork or force through ricer or sieve. Mix in 1 uncooked egg yolk, cider vinegar and dry mustard, in order.
7. Add salad oil very gradually while beating constantly.
8. Mix in parsley, fillets, capers and thyme.
9. Pour dressing over beef and toss lightly to mix thoroughly. Garnish with the chopped egg white.

About 4 servings

Oriental Salad

1½	cups strips of cold roast pork
2	cups sliced Chinese cabbage (celery cabbage)
1	16-oz. can bean sprouts (about 2 cups, drained)
1	5-oz. can water chestnuts
1¾	cups cooked rice
1	cup cooked peas
⅔	cup thick sour cream
⅓	cup mayonnaise
2	tablespoons soy sauce
1	tablespoon cider vinegar
1	teaspoon celery seed
¼	teaspoon garlic salt
¼	teaspoon pepper

1. Cut into thin strips enough cold roast pork to yield 1½ cups.
2. Wash, trim off roots, separate stalks, remove any blemishes and slice enough Chinese cabbage to yield 2 cups.
3. Drain contents of can of bean sprouts and can of water chestnuts.
4. Slice the water chestnuts. Combine the Chinese cabbage, pork, bean sprouts, water chestnuts, rice and peas.
5. Toss lightly to mix. Chill thoroughly in refrigerator.
6. Blend together and chill thoroughly sour cream, mayonnaise, soy sauce, cider vinegar, celery seed, garlic salt and pepper.
7. Just before serving, pour dressing over salad and toss lightly to mix thoroughly. Serve in a salad bowl; garnish with pimiento strips or green pepper strips.

About 8 servings

Sea Food Medley

1	6½-oz. can crab meat (about 1⅓ cups, drained)
2	6-oz. cans lobster meat (about 1½ cups, drained)
1	5-oz. can shrimp (about ¾ cup, drained; remove black veins if present)
3	eggs
1	qt. (about ½ head) shredded lettuce
1	cup diced celery
¼	cup sliced radishes
¼	cup sliced green onions
1	medium-size ripe avocado
2	tablespoons lemon juice
½	cup (about 2 oz.) walnuts
2	medium-size tomatoes, chilled
1	cup mayonnaise
¼	cup cream
1	teaspoon salt
¼	teaspoon pepper

1. Drain, remove and discard bony tissue, and separate contents of can of crab meat.
2. Drain contents of cans of lobster meat and shrimp.
3. Cut lobster and shrimp into pieces. Combine in a bowl with crab meat and chill in refrigerator.
4. Hard-cook eggs and chill.
5. Prepare and put lettuce, celery, radishes and onions into a large salad bowl.
6. Set in refrigerator to chill at least 1 hr.
7. Shortly before serving, prepare avocado and cut into cubes.
8. Coat pieces with lemon juice.
9. Add to the salad bowl. Dice the hard-cooked eggs and add to the salad bowl, together with the sea food. Coarsely chop and add walnuts.
10. Rinse, cut out stem ends, dice and add tomatoes.
11. Mix all ingredients together lightly but thoroughly.
12. Blend together mayonnaise, cream, salt and pepper.
13. Add to salad bowl and toss lightly.

About 12 servings

Note: If desired, reserve lobster meat from claws or use some shrimp to garnish. Or top with **capers, green pepper strips** or **ripe olives. Cooked Sour-Cream Dressing** (page 62) or **Cooked Marshmallow Dressing** (page 72) may be substituted for the mayonnaise mixture.

Vegetable-Pork Salad

2   **cups cold roast pork cubes**
⅔   **cup coarsely grated process American cheese**
½   **cup diced celery**
2   **tablespoons sliced stuffed olives**
1   **cup cooked peas**
⅓   **cup small white cocktail onions**
½   **cup mayonnaise**
1   **teaspoon salt**
⅛   **teaspoon white pepper**

1. Prepare and put into a bowl pork cubes, American cheese, celery and olives.
2. Add and mix lightly peas and onions.
3. Blend together and add mayonnaise, salt and white pepper.
4. Toss lightly to mix thoroughly. Chill in refrigerator.
5. Serve on **curly endive.** Garnish with thin strips of **pimiento.**

About 4 servings

Cooked Shrimp

1   **lb. fresh shrimp with shells**
2   **cups water**
2   **tablespoons lemon juice**
2   **teaspoons salt**
1   **bay leaf**

1. Wash shrimp in cold water.
2. Drop shrimp into a boiling mixture of water, lemon juice, salt and bay leaf.
3. Cover tightly. Simmer 5 min., or only until shrimp are pink and tender. Drain and cover with cold water to chill. Drain shrimp again. Remove tiny legs. Peel shells from shrimp. Cut a slit along back (outer curved surface) of shrimp to expose the black vein. With knife point, remove vein in one piece. Rinse shrimp quickly in cold water. Drain on absorbent paper. Store in refrigerator until ready to use.

About 3 cups shrimp

Note: Veins present in canned or frozen shrimp are removed in the same way.

Shrimp Slaw

1   **lb. fresh shrimp with shells (see Cooked Shrimp, page 36)**
2   **cups shredded cabbage**
1   **cup chopped celery**
⅔   **cup mayonnaise**
2   **tablespoons tarragon vinegar**
2   **tablespoons cream**
2   **tablespoons finely chopped parsley**
2   **tablespoons minced onion**
½   **teaspoon celery seed**
½   **teaspoon basil**
½   **teaspoon salt**
¼   **teaspoon pepper**

1. Cook shrimp and cut into pieces.
2. Prepare cabbage and celery and toss lightly with shrimp.
3. Set in refrigerator to chill.
4. For Dressing—Blend together mayonnaise, vinegar, cream, parsley, onion and a mixture of celery seed, basil, salt and pepper and chill in refrigerator.
5. To serve, pour dressing over shrimp mixture, Toss lightly to mix thoroughly.

About 6 servings

Shrimp and Avocado Salad

1   cup wine vinegar
1/3 cup water
1/2 cup lemon juice
1   cup salad oil
1/4 cup chopped parsley
2   cloves garlic, minced
1   tablespoon salt
1/4 teaspoon freshly ground
    black pepper
1   tablespoon sugar
1   teaspoon dry mustard
1   teaspoon thyme, crushed
1   teaspoon oregano, crushed
2   lbs. large cooked shrimp,
    peeled, and deveined
3   small onions, sliced
1/3 cup chopped green pepper
2   ripe avocados, peeled and
    sliced

1. For marinade, combine vinegar, water, lemon juice, oil, parsley, and garlic in a bowl or a screwtop jar. Add a mixture of salt, pepper, sugar, dry mustard, thyme, and oregano; blend thoroughly.
2. Put shrimp, onions, and green pepper into a large shallow dish. Pour marinade over all, cover and refrigerate 8 hours or overnight.
3. About 1 hour before serving, put avocado slices into bowl. Pour enough marinade from shrimp over the avocado to cover completely.
4. To serve, remove avocado slices and shrimp from marinade and arrange on crisp **lettuce** in a large serving bowl.

About 8 servings

Luscious Rock Lobster Salad

3   6- to 8-oz. frozen rock
    lobster tails (or use 3
    6-oz. cans rock lobster
    meat)
1 1/2 qts. water
1 1/2 teaspoons salt
1   cup diced celery
1/2 cup slivered unblanched
    almonds
1   tablespoon minced
    scallions or onion
3/4 cup mayonnaise
2   tablespoons cream
2   tablespoons lemon juice
1/4 teaspoon sugar
1/4 teaspoon salt
1/4 teaspoon crushed dried
    tarragon leaves
1/8 teaspoon white pepper

1. If using canned rock lobster, chill in the can in refrigerator. Drain and cut into chunks when ready to prepare salad.
2. To Cook Frozen Rock Lobster Tails—Bring water and salt to boiling in a heavy sauce pot or kettle.
3. Add frozen or thawed rock lobster tails to kettle. Cover; bring water again to boiling, reduce heat and simmer for 7 to 12 min.
4. Drain tails, cover with cold water and drain again. Using scissors or a sharp knife, cut through thin shell or underside of each tail. Insert fingers under meat and carefully pull it out. Cool meat; chill in refrigerator. Cut into chunks when ready to prepare salad.
5. To Complete Salad—Prepare celery, almonds and minced scallions or onion.
6. Put into a large bowl, reserving about 2 tablespoons of the almonds for garnish. Add the rock lobster meat.
7. Blend together mayonnaise, cream, lemon juice, sugar, 1/4 teaspoon salt, tarragon leaves and white pepper.
8. Add to the ingredients in the bowl, toss lightly to mix thoroughly. Chill.
9. Serve in a chilled salad bowl; garnish with reserved almonds and **ripe olives.**

6 servings

Lobster Paradise

	Russian Dressing (page 63)
2	**cups (2 6-oz. cans) chilled lobster meat, cut into pieces (or use cooked fresh lobster meat)**
2	**serving bowls (each large enough to hold crushed ice and pineapple half)**
1	**medium-size fresh pineapple, chilled**
	Crushed ice
4	**Carrot Curls**
2	**Green Pepper Rings**
2	**thin lemon or lime slices**
4	**teaspoons finely chopped celery**
4	**thin strips of pimiento**
¼	**teaspoon chopped pimiento**
¼	**teaspoon chopped ripe olives**
2	**teaspoons capers**
	Ripe or green olives
1	**teaspoon caviar**

1. Prepare and chill Russian Dressing.
2. For two servings, have lobster meat, serving bowls, pineapple and crushed ice ready.
3. Prepare **pineapple shells.** Cut part of the fruit into small, thin slices. Reserve remaining pineapple for use in other food preparation.
4. Prepare and set aside carrots curls, pepper rings, lemon or lime slices, celery, pimiento and ripe olives.
5. Set out capers.
6. Toss the lobster meat lightly with some of the pineapple pieces. Spoon mixture into shells. Arrange the remainder of the pineapple pieces around the lobster mixture.
7. Fill the bowls with crushed ice. Arrange the filled shells on the ice beds. Garnish the lobster mixture with green pepper rings. Spoon the celery into the green pepper rings and top with the capers. Lay the pimiento strips crosswise over the rings. Put the lemon or lime slices at the base of each pineapple crown and garnish slices with the chopped pimiento and olive. Arrange on the ice beds, at both ends of each pineapple, carrot curls and ripe or green olives.
8. Just before serving, garnish dressing with caviar.
9. Serve the salad immediately with the dressing.

2 servings

Crab Meat Salad

2	**6½-oz. cans crab meat (about 2⅔ cups, drained)**
½	**cup diced celery**
⅔	**cup mayonnaise**
⅛	**teaspoon pepper**
	Lemon or lime wedges

1. Drain, remove and discard bony tissue, and separate contents of cans of crab meat.
2. Prepare and mix diced celery with crab meat.
3. Mix together and add mayonnaise and pepper.
4. Toss lightly to mix thoroughly. Chill in refrigerator.
5. When ready to serve, pile salad lightly in lettuce cups (page 21). Serve with lemon or lime wedges.

About 4 servings

Curried Crab Meat Salad: Follow recipe for Crab Meat Salad. Mix ½ cup chopped **ripe olives** and/or ⅔ cup coarsely chopped toasted, blanched **almonds** with the celery. Omit the pepper, increase the mayonnaise to 1 cup and blend in 2 teaspoons **lemon juice** and 1 teaspoon **curry powder.** If desired, while salad is chilling, prepare and chill 4 **Tomato Shells** (page 23). When ready to serve, lightly fill the shells with salad mixture.

Salmon Salad in Grapefruit Baskets

2   **medium-size grapefruit**
1   **16-oz. can salmon (about 2 cups, flaked)**
½   **cup diced celery**
½   **cup mayonnaise**
¼   **cup chili sauce**
1   **teaspoon grated onion**

1. Prepare Grapefruit Baskets (page 12), reserving and draining pulp from grapefruit.
2. Drain, flake and put salmon into a bowl.
3. Add drained grapefruit pulp to the salmon with celery.
4. Toss together lightly.
5. Blend together mayonnaise, chili sauce and grated onion and pour over salad mixture.
6. Toss lightly to mix thoroughly. Chill in refrigerator to allow flavors to blend.
7. When ready to serve, heap salad carefully into the grapefruit shells.

4 servings

Tuna Salad

2   **7-oz. cans tuna (about 2 cups, drained)**
1   **cup sliced celery**
¼   **cup sliced radishes**
2   **tablespoons chopped green pepper**
½   **cup salad dressing**
1   **tablespoon lemon juice**
1   **tablespoon minced onion**
¼   **teaspoon pepper**
    Crisp salad greens

1. Drain tuna well and separate into small chunks and put into a bowl.
2. Prepare celery, radishes and green pepper and mix lightly with the tuna.
3. Blend together and add salad dressing, lemon juice, onion and pepper.
4. Toss lightly to mix thoroughly.
5. Chill mixture thoroughly in refrigerator.
6. To serve, arrange crisp salad greens on a chilled serving plate or in a salad bowl.
7. Spoon the tuna salad in the center. Garnish with strips of **pimiento.**

About 4 servings

Tuna-Cheese Salad: Follow recipe for Tuna Salad. Omit celery and radishes. Toss tuna lightly with 1½ cups (about 6 oz.) shredded **Swiss cheese.** Increase salad dressing to about 1 cup. Before serving, add ⅔ cup coarsely chopped **cashew nuts** and mix lightly.

Tuna Salad Piquant: Follow recipe for Tuna Salad. Omit celery, radishes and onion. Toss tuna lightly with ½ cup small white **cocktail onions.** Blend ¼ cup **chili sauce** with salad dressing mixture.

Tuna-Apple Salad: Follow recipe for Tuna Salad. Omit radishes and salad dressing mixture. Mix 2 cups (about 2 medium size) diced red **apple,** unpared, with the tuna. Toss salad lightly with about ⅔ cup **Curry** and **Mayonnaise** (page 63).

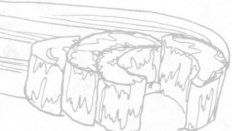

Stewed Chicken

1   **stewing chicken, 4 to 5 lbs. ready-to-cook weight**
    Hot water to barely cover
1   **small onion**
3   **sprigs parsley**
2   **3-in. pieces celery with leaves**
1   **bay leaf**
3   **peppercorns**
2   **teaspoons salt**

1. Set out a kettle or sauce pot having a tight-fitting cover.
2. Clean chicken (If chicken is frozen, thaw according to directions on package.)
3. Disjoint and cut into serving-size pieces. Rinse chicken pieces and giblets. Refrigerate the liver. Put chicken pieces, gizzard, heart and neck into the kettle and add hot water to barely cover.
4. Add to water onion, parsley, celery with leaves, bay leaf, peppercorns and salt.
5. Bring water to boiling; remove foam. Cover kettle tightly, reduce heat and simmer chicken 1 hr., skimming foam from surface as necessary. Continue cooking chicken 1 to 2 hrs. longer, or until thickest pieces are tender when pierced with a fork. During last 15 min. of cooking time, add liver to kettle.
6. Remove chicken and giblets from broth. Cool chicken slightly and remove skin. Remove meat from bones. Cut meat into pieces as directed in recipes. Strain broth and cool slightly. Remove fat that rises to surface. Refrigerate fat and broth and use in other food preparation. Unless using meat immediately, cool, cover and refrigerate.

About 3 to 3½ cups diced chicken

Chicken Salad De Luxe

3   **cups cooked chicken cubes (see Stewed Chicken, above)**
1   **cup diced celery**
½   **cup small seedless grapes (or use green grapes cut into halves and seeded)**
½   **cup (2 to 3 oz.) toasted pecans or toasted blanched almonds, chopped**
¼   **cup (1 oz.) moist shredded coconut, cut fine**
¼   **cup chilled whipping cream**
¾   **cup Cooked Salad Dressing (page 61)**

1. Set a small bowl and rotary beater in refrigerator to chill.
2. Prepare and put chicken cubes and celery into a large bowl.
3. Rinse grapes, drain, and add to bowl.
4. Set in refrigerator to chill.
5. Prepare pecans or coconut and set aside.
6. Before serving, using chilled bowl and beater, beat whipping cream until of medium consistency (piles softly).
7. Blend the whipped cream into ¾ cup Cooked Salad Dressing.
8. Lightly toss nuts and coconut with chicken mixture. Add salad dressing mixture; toss gently to coat evenly.

About 6 servings

Note: Cooked **Sour-Cream Dressing** (page 62) or **Cooked Marshmallow Dressing** (page 72) may be substituted for the salad dressing mixture.

Chicken-Curry Salad: Follow recipe for Chicken Salad De Luxe. Blend ½ to 1 teaspoon **curry powder** into the salad dressing mixture.

Chicken-Roquefort Salad: Follow recipe for Chicken Salad De Luxe. Substitute 2 cups shredded **lettuce** for celery. Omit grapes and coconut. Increase salad dressing to 1 cup and blend in 1½ oz. **Roquefort cheese,** crumbled.

Turkey Salad: Follow recipe for Chicken Salad De Luxe or any variation. Substitute cooked **turkey** for chicken.

Macaroni-Frank Salad Bowl

Macaroni (one-half recipe, page 9; add 1 small clove garlic and 1 small onion to the water)
1   **cup thick sour cream**
¼   **cup French dressing (page 64)**
½   **teaspoon salt**
2   **medium-size tomatoes**
2   **cups curly endive pieces**
1   **cup diced celery**
¼   **cup thinly sliced radishes**
¼   **cup sliced green onions**
2   **frankfurters, sliced**

1. Prepare macaroni.
2. Remove and discard garlic and onion.
3. Blend hot macaroni with sour cream, French dressing and salt.
4. Set in refrigerator to chill thoroughly.
5. Rinse tomatoes, peel, cut into wedges and chill.
6. Rinse and tear into pieces enough curly endive to yield 2 cups.
7. Put into a large salad bowl with celery, radishes, green onions and frankfuters.
8. Add the macaroni mixture and tomato wedges to salad bowl and toss lightly to mix thoroughly.

6 to 8 servings

Macaroni Picnic Salad

1   **pkg. (16 oz.) elbow macaroni (4 cups)**
1   **cup each sliced radishes, sliced celery and sliced sweet gherkins**
2   **tablespoons chopped onion**
1   **cup mayonnaise**
⅓   **cup sweet pickle liquid**
¼   **cup spicy brown mustard**
1   **teaspoon prepared horseradish**
1   **teaspoon salt**
⅛   **teaspoon white pepper**

1. Cook macaroni in boiling salted water following directions on package.
2. Drain in colander.
3. Combine the macaroni in a large bowl with radishes, celery, sweet gherkins and chopped onion.
4. Mix mayonnaise, sweet pickle liquid, brown mustard, horseradish, salt, and white pepper thoroughly in a small bowl.
5. Toss dressing with macaroni mixture. Chill.
6. When ready to serve salad, garnish with **salad greens, radish roses** and **gherkin fans.**

About 8 servings

Avocado Crab Salad, Paella Style

2 cans (5 oz. each) lobster (or use fresh lobster)
2 doz. small clams*
¾ lb. fresh shrimp
1 clove garlic, crushed
1 tablespoon butter or margarine
2 tablespoons dry sherry
¼ teaspoon saffron, crushed
Dash pepper
1¼ cups uncooked rice
¾ cup small pimiento-stuffed olives
2 ripe avocados

1. Drain and remove bones from lobster (see note below).
2. Cook clams gently in boiling salted water to cover until the shells open.
3. Remove clams and cook shrimp, in the same liquid 3 to 5 min., covered.
4. Chill the shellfish, strain and measure 2½ cups of the fish broth into a medium sauce pan. Add garlic, butter or margarine, dry sherry, saffron, and pepper.
5. Bring to boiling and add uncooked rice.
6. Cover and cook over low heat about 15 min., or until rice kernels are soft and broth is absorbed.
7. Shell the chilled shrimp. (If using freshly cooked lobster, shell and cut meat into pieces; reserve 2 claws for garnish.)
8. Combine rice, clams, shrimp and lobster in a large mixing bowl. Add pimiento-stuffed olives.
9. Mix lightly with a fork and chill thoroughly.
10. When ready to serve avocados, peel, halve, remove seeds and brush lightly with lemon juice.
11. Turn salad mixture into serving bowl and arrange avocado, cut in wedges, over top. (Garnish with lobster claws, if available.)
12. Serve the salad with **olive oil, herbed mayonnaise, salad dressing** or **tartar sauce,** as desired.

6 to 8 servings

Note: If using fresh lobster meat, cook lobsters (about 1¼ lbs. each) in 3 qts. boiling water and 3 tablespoons salt. Cover pot and cook lobsters over low heat about 20 min. Remove lobsters and use the same liquid to cook the clams and shrimp (one shellfish at a time). Reserve the cooking liquid.

*If desired, 1 doz. mussels may be substituted for 1 doz. small clams.

Shrimp Salad with Coral Dressing

2 cups cooked, peeled, and deveined shrimp
1½ cups cooked rice
½ cup sliced celery
½ cup chopped unpeeled cucumbers
¼ cup chopped chives
⅓ cup mayonnaise
¼ cup dairy sour cream
1 tablespoon chili sauce
¼ teaspoon onion salt
⅛ teaspoon pepper
1½ teaspoons tarragon vinegar
Salad greens
Horseradish (optional)
Lemon wedges

1. Toss shrimp, rice, celery, cucumbers, and chives together.
2. Blend ingredients for dressing. Pour over shrimp Mixture and toss thoroughly. Chill.
3. Serve on salad greens. Top with a little horseradish, if desired, and garnish with lemon wedges.
4. Accompany with cahmpagne.

6 servings

Molded Salads

To turn out a salad mold that is shapely and unscarred by removal from the mold, and that has solid ingredients distributed throughout, a few simple techniques should be followed.

Lightly oil molds, brushing them with a tasteless salad or cooking oil; do not use olive oil, which has a distinctive flavor. Turn the mold upside down on absorbent paper to let any excess oil drain off.

Chill gelatin mixtures either by setting the bowl in the refrigerator or by putting it in a pan containing ice and water. If placed in the refrigerator, stir occasionally; if placed over ice and water (a quicker method), stir frequently. If the gelatin mixture is clear, chill until slightly thicker than consistency of thick, unbeaten egg white before adding any solid ingredients. If the mixture contains ingredients which thicken it or make it opaque, chill until it begins to gel (gets slightly thicker); mix in solid ingredients only after mixture begins to gel.

Unmold gelatin by first running the tip of a knife around the top edge to loosen it and admit air; then invert the mold on a chilled plate. If the mold cannot be lifted off immediately, wet a clean towel in hot water, quickly wring it almost dry, and wrap the hot towel around the mold for a few seconds. Repeat if necessary.

Party-Perfect Salad Molds

1 pkg. (10 oz.) frozen sliced peaches
½ cup drained maraschino cherries, sliced
¼ cup (about 1½ oz.) blanched almonds, chopped
1 3-oz. pkg. orange-flavored gelatin
   Water (enough to make ¾ cup liquid)
1 cup ginger ale
¼ cup lemon juice

1. Set out six ½-cup individual molds. Set out peaches to thaw according to directions on package.
2. Prepare cherries and almonds and set aside.
3. Drain the peaches (about 1 cup, drained), reserving syrup in a 1-cup measuring cup for liquids.
4. Empty gelatin into a bowl.
5. Add water (enough to make ¾ cup liquid) to the reserved peach syrup, if necessary.
6. Heat until very hot. Add to bowl land stir until gelatin is completely dissolved. Stir in ginger ale and lemon juice.
7. Cool; chill until mixture is slightly thicker than consistency of thick, unbeaten egg white.
8. Lightly oil the molds with salad or cooking oil (not olive oil); set aside to drain.
9. When gelatin mixture is of desired consistency, stir in the peaches, cherries and almonds. Turn into the prepared molds and chill in refrigerator until firm.
10. Unmold (on this page) onto chilled salad plates. Garnish with sprigs of water cress.

6 servings

Mandarin Orange Mold: Follow recipe for Party-Perfect Salad Molds. Use a 1-qt. mold instead of the individual molds. Substitute two 11-oz. cans **mandarin oranges,** drained, for the peaches and the **orange syrup** for the peach syrup. Increase the syrup and water mixture to 1 cup; omit the lemon juice.

Molded Avocado-Kumquat Salad

1 3-oz. pkg. lemon-flavored gelatin
¾ cup very hot water
1¼ cups ginger ale
¼ teaspoon salt
1 pt. kumquats (about 2 cups, sliced)
1½ cups (about 2 small) diced avocado

1. Set out a 1-qt. mold.
2. Empty gelatin int a bowl.
3. Add water and stir until gelatin is completely dissolved.
4. Stir in ginger ale and salt.
5. Cool; chill until mixture is slighly thicker than consistency of thick, unbeaten egg white.
6. Lightly oil the mold with salad or cooking oil (not olive oil); set aside to drain.
7. Remove leaves, rinse, drain and thinly slice kumquats.
8. Prepare avocado.
9. When gelatin mixture is of desired consistency, mix in the kumquats and avocado. Turn into the prepared mold and chill in refrigerator until firm.
10. Unmold onto chilled serving plate.

6 to 8 servings

Molded Avocado-Grapefruit Salad: Follow recipe for Molded Avocado-Kumquat Salad. Increase hot water to 1½ cups and substitute ½ cup **grapefruit juice** for ginger ale. Substitute 1 cup **grapefruit sections,** cut into halves, for kumquat slices.

Cranberry Ring-Around-Grapefruit Mold

½	cup cold water
2	env. unflavored gelatin
4	cups (2 16-oz. cans) whole cranberry sauce
¼	cup orange juice
2	teaspoons grated orange peel
½	cup (about 2 oz.) pecans
16	(¼ lb.) marshmallows
	Grapefruit sections

1. Set out a 1½-qt. ring mold.
2. Pour water into a small bowl.
3. Sprinkle gelatin evenly over water.
4. Let stand until gelatin is softened. Dissolve completely by placing bowl over very hot water.
5. Meanwhile, combine cranberry sauce, orange juice and orange peel in a bowl and blend thoroughly.
6. When gelatin is dissolved, blend into the cranberry mixture. Chill until mixture begins to gel (gets slightly thicker).
7. Lightly oil the mold with salad or cooking oil (not olive oil); set aside to drain.
8. Chop pecans and set aside.
9. Cut marshmallows into small pieces.
10. Set aside.
11. When gelatin mixture is of desired consistency, stir in the nuts. Spoon one half of the gelatin mixture into the mold. Top with marshmallow pieces. Spoon in the remaining gelatin mixture. Chill in refrigerator until firm.
12. Unmold onto chilled platter. Fill center with grapefruit sections.
13. If desired, garnish with few springs of **mint**.

8 to 10 servings

Pomegranate Star Mold

5	pomegranates
1¾	cups water
2	¼-in. slices lemon
1	cup cold water
3	env. unflavored gelatin
¾	cup sugar
2	tablespoons grenadine
½	teaspoon red food coloring

1. Lightly oil a 1½-qt. star-shaped mold with salad or cooking oil (not olive oil); set aside to drain.
2. Cut into halves and remove seeds and juice from pomegranates.
3. Put seeds and juice into a saucepan with 1¾ cups water and lemon.
4. Bring to boiling, cover and simmer for 15 min., or until the color and flavor of seeds have been absorbed by the water.
5. Meanwhile, pour water into a small bowl.
6. Sprinkle gelatin evenly over water.
7. Let stand until softened.
8. Turn hot mixture into a sieve or food mill set over a saucepan. Discard lemon slices; force pomegranate mixture through the sieve or food mill until all juice has been extracted. Discard the pomegranate seeds.
9. Reheat the pomegranate juice until very hot. Remove from heat and immediately stir in softened gelatin until gelatin is completely dissolved. Stir in sugar until dissolved.
10 Blend in grenadine and food coloring.
11. Pour into the mold. Cool; chill in refrigerator until firm.
12. Unmold onto a chilled serving plate. Garnish with curly endive.

8 servings

Citrus-Pecan Mold

½   cup lime juice
2   env. unflavored gelatin
1¼   cups orange juice
⅔   cup sugar
¼   teaspoon salt
2   cups ginger ale
2   cups orange sections
⅔   cup (about 2½ oz.) pecans

1. Set out a 1½-qt. mold.
2. Pour lime juice into a small bowl.
3. Sprinkle gelatin evenly over lime juice.
4. Let stand until softened.
5. Heat orange juice until very hot.
6. Remove from heat and immediately stir in softened gelatin until gelatin is completely dissolved. Stir in sugar, salt and ginger ale in order.
7. Cool; chill until mixture is slightly thicker than consistency of thick, unbeaten egg white.
8. Lightly oil the mold with salad or cooking oil (not olive oil); set aside to drain.
9. Prepare and section enough oranges to yield 2 cups.
10. Coarsely chop pecans and set aside.
11. When gelatin mixture is of desired consistency, mix in the orange sections and pecans. Turn into the mold; chill in refrigerator until firm.
12. Unmold onto chilled serving plate.

8 to 10 servings

Layered Apple-Cranberry Salad

1   3-oz. pkg. lime-flavored gelatin
1   cup very hot water
1   cup thick sweetened applesauce
½   cup apple juice
1   3-oz. pkg. cherry-flavored gelatin
1   cup very hot water
½   cup (about 2 oz.) pecans
2   cups (16-oz. can) whole cranberry sauce

1. Lightly oil a 1½-qt. mold with salad or cooking oil (not olive oil); set aside to drain.
2. For Apple Layer—Empty gelatin into a bowl.
3. Add and stir water until gelatin is completely dissolved.
4. Stir in applesauce and apple juice.
5. Pour into prepared mold. Cool; chill in refrigerator until partially set.
6. For Cranberry Layer—Empty gelatin into a bowl.
7. Add and stir water until gelatin is completely dissolved.
8. Cool; chill until gelatin mixture is slightly thicker than consistency of thick, unbeaten egg white.
9. Meanwhile, chop pecans.
10. Set out cranberry sauce.
11. When the second gelatin mixture is of desired consistency, stir in the pecans and cranberry sauce.
12. When first layer in mold is partially set, immediately turn the cranberry mixture into the mold. (Both layers should be of almost the same consistency when combined to avoid separation when unmolded.) Chill in refrigerator until firm.
13. Unmold onto a chilled serving plate.

8 to 10 servings

Molded Cranberry Salads

2 cups cranberries
1 medium-size orange
½ lemon
1 cup sugar
   Water (enough to make 2 cups liquid)
2 3-oz. pkgs. raspberry- or cherry-flavored gelatin (or use 1 3-oz. pkg. of either flavor and 1 3-oz. pkg. lemon-flavored gelatin)
2 cups very hot water

1. Set out eight ¾-cup individual molds.
2. For Cranberry Relish—Wash and sort cranberries.
3. Rinse (do not peel), cut into pieces and, if necessary, remove seeds from orange and lemon.
4. Put the fruit through the medium blade of a food chopper. Blend in sugar.
5. Cover; chill in refrigerator at least 1 hr. to allow flavors to blend.
6. For Salad—When cranberry relish is chilled, drain, reserving syrup in a 2-cup measuring cup for liquids. Add water (enough to make 2 cups liquid) to the syrup.
7. Empty gelatin into a large bowl.
8. Add and stir 2 cups very hot water until gelatin is completely dissolved.
9. Stir in the syrup mixture. Cool; chill until gelatin mixture is slightly thicker than consistency of thick, unbeaten egg white.
10. Lightly oil the molds with salad or cooking oil (not olive oil); set aside to drain.
11. When gelatin mixture is of desired consistency, blend in the cranberry relish. Turn into the prepared molds and chill in refrigerator until firm.
12. Unmold onto chilled individual salad plates lined with crisp salad greens.

8 servings

Cranberry-Apple Salads: Follow recipe for Molded Cranberry Salads. Substitute for the one-half lemon 1 **apple,** rinsed, quartered, cored and coarsely chopped (do not put through food chopper).

Cranberry-Walnut Salads: Follow recipe for Molded Cranberry Salads or recipe for Cranberry-Apple Salads; mix in ½ cup (about 2 oz.) chopped **walnuts** with the cranberry relish.

Two-Layer Waldorf Salad

2   **3-oz. pkgs. lemon-flavored gelatin**
2   **cups very hot water**
1   **cup cold water**
¼   **cup lime juice**
1   **medium-size red apple**
½   **cup chopped celery**
½   **cup (about 2 oz.) chopped walnuts**
⅔   **cup mayonnaise**
    Crips curly endive

1. Lightly oil a 1½-qt. fancy mold with salad or cooking oil (not olive oil); set aside to drain.
2. Empty gelatin into a bowl.
3. Add and stir 2 cups very hot water until gelatin is completely dissolved.
4. Stir in 1 cup cold water and lime juice.
5. Cool. Pour about one third of the gelatin mixture into the prepared mold. Chill in refrigerator until partially set.
6. Chill remaining gelatin mixture until slightly thicker than consistency of thick, unbeaten egg white.
7. Meanwhile, wash quarter, core and chop apple.
8. Prepare celery and walnuts.
9. When second gelatin mixture is of desired consistency, blend in mayonnaise.
10. Add and mix in the apple, celery and walnuts.
11. When first layer in mold is partially set, immediately spoon the fruit-gelatin mixture over it. (Both layers should be of almost the same consistency when combined to avoid separation when unmolded.) Chill in refrigerator until firm.
12. Unmold onto chilled serving plate. Garnish with crisp curly endive.

8 to 10 servings

Apricot Luncheon Mold

⅔   **cup undiluted evaporated milk**
1   **8¾-oz. can apricot halves (7 to 10 halves)**
    Water (enough to make 1 cup liquid)
1   **3-oz. pkg. lemon-flavored gelatin**
2   **tablespoons lemon juice**
½   **cup diced celery**
½   **cup (about 2 oz.) chopped pecans**
1½   **cups cream-style cottage cheese**

1. Set out a 1-qt. ring mold. Set a bowl and rotary beater in refrigerator to chill.
2. Chill evaporated milk in freezing compartment of refrigerator until icy cold.
3. Drain apricot halves reserving syrup.
4. Add water to the reserved apricot syrup.
5. Heat until very hot.
6. Empty gelatin into a bowl.
7. Add the hot liquid and stir until gelatin is completely dissolved. Stir in lemon juice.
8. Cool; chill until mixture is slightly thicker than consistency of thick, unbeaten egg white.
9. Lightly oil the mold with salad or cooking oil (not olive oil); set aside to drain.
10. Prepare celery and pecans.
11. When gelatin mixture is of desired consistency, blend in the celery, pecans and cottage cheese.
12. Using chilled bowl and beater, beat the chilled evaporated milk until very stiff. Gently fold into gelatin mixture. Arrange apricot halves, cut side up in bottom of mold, Carefully turn the gelatin mixture into the mold and chill in refrigerator until firm.
13. Unmold onto a chilled serving plate. Garnish with **curly endive.**

About 6 servings

Cherry Salad Ring

½ cup maraschino cherries
1 20-oz. can crushed pineapple (about 1¾ cups, drained)
½ cup cold water
1 env. unflavored gelatin
½ cup very hot water
¼ cup lime juice
8 oz. cream cheese, softened

1. Lightly oil a 1-qt. ring mold with salad or cooking oil (not olive oil); set aside to drain.
2. Coarsely chop maraschino cherries and set aside on absorbent paper to drain. (To avoid a pink tint in the salad, drain cherries thoroughly.)
3. Drain pineapple thoroughly, reserving syrup.
4. Pour ½ cup cold water into a small cup or custard cup.
5. Sprinkle gelatin evenly over water.
6. Let stand until softened.
7. Stir the softened gelatin into ½ cup very hot water.
8. Stir until completely dissolved. Blend in ¾ cup reserved pineapple syrup and lime juice.
9. Arrange about 2 tablespoons maraschino cherries in bottom of the mold. Pour in a small amount of gelatin mixture. (just enough to cover the cherries). Chill in refrigerator until partially set.
10. Chill remaining gelatin mixture until slightly thicker than consistency of thick, unbeaten egg white.
11. Meanwhile, beat cream cheese until fluffy.
12. Add gradually and beat in the remaining pineapple syrup.
13. When gelatin mixture is about the same consistency as cheese mixture; stir several tablespoons into the cheese mixture slowly, beating constantly until well blended. Stir in pineapple and remaining cherries.
14. When first layer in mold is of desired consistency, spoon the cheese mixture over it, spreading evenly. (Both layers should be of almost the same consistency when combined to avoid separation when unmolded.) Chill in refrigerator until firm.
15. Unmold onto chilled plate; garnish.

6 to 8 servings

Peaches and Cream Salad

1 29-oz. can sliced peaches (about 2 cups, drained)
1 3-oz. pkg. lemon-flavored gelatin
⅔ cup cream-style cottage cheese
½ cup (2 oz.) salted pecans, chopped
½ cup chilled whipping cream

1. Set out a 1-qt. mold.
2. Drain peaches, reserving syrup.
3. Heat 1 cup of the syrup until very hot.
4. Meanwhile, empty gelatin into a bowl.
5. Add the hot peach syrup and stir until gelatin is completely dissolved. Cool; chill until gelatin mixture is slightly thicker than consistency of thick, unbeaten egg white.
6. Lightly oil the mold with salad or cooking oil (not olive oil); set aside to drain. Set a bowl and rotary beater in refrigerator to chill.
7. When gelatin mixture is of desired consistency, mix in the peaches, cottage cheese and pecans.
8. Using the chilled bowl and beater, beat ½ cup chilled whipping cream until cream is of medium consistency (piles softly).
9. Fold whipped cream into gelatin mixture. Turn into the prepared mold and chill in refrigerator until firm. Unmold and garnish.

6 to 8 servings

Avocado Crab Salad, Paella Style 42

Molded Pineapple-Cheese Salad

1 **20-oz. can crushed pineapple (about 1¾ cups, drained)**
2 **env. unflavored gelatin**
  Water to make ¾ cup liquid
½ **cup sugar**
½ **teaspoon salt**
1 **cup unsweetened pineapple juice**
1 **cup orange juice**
2 **or 3 drops yellow food coloring**
2 **8-oz. pkgs. cream cheese, softened**
3 **tablespoons lemon juice**
2 **teaspoons grated lemon peel**
  Frosted Grapes (page 12)
  Mint leaves

1. Set out a 2-qt. ring mold.
2. Drain pineapple and set aside. Reserve syrup.
3. Pour ½ cup of the reserved syrup and ¼ cup cold water into a small bowl. Sprinkle gelatin evenly over surface.
4. Let stand until softened.
5. Add water to remaining pineapple syrup.
6. Heat until boiling. Remove from heat and immediately stir in softened gelatin until gelatin is completely dissolved. Add sugar and salt stirring until dissolved.
7. Stir in pineapple juice, orange juice and food coloring.
8. Cool; chill until mixture is slightly thicker than consistency of thick, unbeaten egg white.
9. Lightly oil the mold with salad or cooking oil (not olive oil); set aside to drain.
10. Beat cream cheese until fluffy.
11. Add lemon juice and lemon peel gradually.
12. When gelatin mixture is about the same consistency as the cheese mixture, stir several tablespoonfuls into cheese mixture. Continue to add gelatin mixture slowly, beating constantly, until well blended. Blend in the crushed pineapple. Turn into prepared mold and chill in refrigerator until firm.
13. Unmold onto chilled serving plate. If desired, fill center of salad ring with **honey-dew melon balls.** Garnish with frosted grapes and mint leaves.
14. Serve with **Pineapple Salad Dressing** (page 70) or **Orange Fruit-Salad Dressing** (page 71).

10 to 12 servings

Layered Fruit-Cheese Buffet Salad

1 **17-oz. can pitted dark sweet cherries (about 1¼ cups, drained)**
  Water (enough to make 1 cup liquid)
1 **3-oz. pkg. cherry-flavored gelatin**
1 **cup very hot water**
1 **30-oz. can peeled apricot halves (about 2 cups, drained)**
1 **17-oz. can pear halves (about 6 halves)**
1 **17-oz. can sliced peaches (about 1¼ cups, drained)**

1. Set out a 3-qt. ring mold.
2. For Cherry Layer—Drain thoroughly, reserving syrup in a 1-cup measuring cup for liquids, the contents of can of pitted dark sweet cherries.
3. Add water (enough to make 1 cup liquid) to the reserved cherry syrup, if necessary.
4. Empty gelatin into a bowl.
5. Add and stir 1 cup very hot water until gelatin is completely dissolved.
6. Stir in the reserved liquid. Cool; chill until mixture is slightly thicker than consistency of thick, unbeaten egg white.
7. Lightly oil the mold with salad or cooking oil (not olive oil); set aside to drain.
8. When gelatin mixture is of desired consistency, stir in the

1   8¼-oz. can crushed pineapple (about ¾ cup, drained)
¼   cup cold water
¼   cup reserved fruit syrup
1   env. unflavored gelatin
½   cup finely chopped celery
¼   cup (about 1 oz.) finely chopped pecans
2   tablespoons minced green pepper
6   oz. cream cheese, softened
1   3-oz. pkg. lemon-flavored gelatin
     Water (enough to make 2 cups liquid)
2   medium-size oranges
2   small red apples

cherries. Turn into prepared mold and chill in refrigerator until partially set.

9. For Cheese Layer—Drain, combining and reserving the syrups, contents of can peeled apricot, can pear halves and can sliced peaches.

10. Cut the fruit into pieces and put into a bowl. Set aside to use in Mixed Fruit Layer.

11. Drain, reserving syrup, contents of can of crushed pineapple.

12. Set the drained pineapple aside.

13. Stir the pineapple syrup into the mixed fruit syrups and set aside.

14. Pour cold water and fruit syrup into a small cup or custard cup.

15. Sprinkle unflavored gelatin evenly over water.

16. Let stand until softened.

17. Prepare celery, pecans and green pepper.

18. Heat 1 cup of the reserved fruit syrup until very hot. Remove from heat and immediately stir in softened gelatin until gelatin is completely dissolved. Cool; chill until gelatin mixture is slightly thicker than consistency of thick, unbeaten egg white.

19. Meanwhile, beat cream cheese until fluffy.

20. When gelatin mixture is about the same consistency as the cheese, stir several tablespoonfuls into the cheese. Continue to add gelatin mixture slowly, beating constantly until well blend. Stir in the drained pineapple, celery, pecans and green pepper.

21. When first layer in mold is partially set, immediately spoon the cheese mixture over it, spreading evenly. (Both layers should be of almost the same consistency when combined to avoid separation when unmolded.) Chill in refrigerator until cheese layer is partially set.

22. For Mixed Fruit Layer—Empty lemon flavored gelatin into a bowl.

23. Measure remaining fruit syrup; if necessary add water (enough to make 2 cups liquid).

24. Heat 1 cup of the liquid until very hot; add to bowl and stir until gelatin is completely dissolved. Stir in the remaining liquid. Cool; chill until mixture is slightly thicker than consistency of thick, unbeaten egg white.

25. Meanwhile, prepare, section and cut oranges into small pieces.

26. Wash apples, quarter, core and cut into small pieces.

27. Mix oranges and apples with reserved fruit in the bowl.

28. When gelatin mixture is of desired consistency, stir in the fruit.

29. Turn mixture into the mold over the cheese layer. Chill in refrigerator until firm.

30. Unmold onto a chilled serving plate.

14 to 16 servings

Dark Sweet Cherry Salad Mold:

Follow recipe for Cherry Layer only. Substitute a 1-qt. mold for the 3-qt. ring mold and **lemon flavored gelatin** for the cherry-flavored gelatin. Add a few drops **red food coloring** with the syrup mixture. Cut the cherries into halves. Stir in ½ cup sliced **stuffed olives** and ½ cup (about 2 oz.) chopped **walnuts** with the cherries. Chill until firm. Unmold.

6 to 8 servings

Mustard Relish Mold

1	cup cold water
2	env. unflavored gelatin
6	eggs
1½	cups sugar
1½	tablespoons dry mustard
1¼	teaspoons salt
1½	cups cider vinegar
1	17-oz. can peas (about 1¾ cups, drained)
1	cup grated carrot (about 2 medium-size)
1	cup chopped celery
1	tablespoon minced parsley
	Curly endive or other crisp greens

1. Set out a 1½-qt. ring mold.
2. Pour water into a small bowl.
3. Sprinkle gelatin evenly over water.
4. Let stand until softened.
5. Beat eggs lightly in top of a double boiler.
6. Combine and blend well sugar, mustard and salt and stir into eggs in double boiler.
7. Add cider vinegar gradually, stirring constantly.
8. Cook over simmering water, stirring constantly, until mixture thickens. Remove from simmering water and immediately add softened gelatin, stirring until gelatin is completely dissolved.
9. Cool; chill until mixture begins to gel (gets slightly thicker).
10. Meanwhile, drain peas.
11. Lightly oil the mold with salad or cooking oil (not olive oil); set aside to drain.
12. Wash, pare or scrape, and grate enough carrots to yield 1 cup.
13. Prepare celery and parsley.
14. When gelatin mixture is of desired consistency, mix in the vegetables. Turn into the prepared mold and chill in refrigerator until firm.
15. Unmold onto chilled serving plate. Garnish with curly endive or other crisp greens.

8 to 10 servings

Tomato Aspic

4	cups tomato juice
⅓	cup chopped celery leaves
⅓	cup chopped onion
2½	tablespoons sugar
1¼	teaspoons salt
1	bay leaf
½	cup cold water
2	env. unflavored gelatin
2½	tablespoons cider vinegar

1. Set out a 1-qt. mold.
2. Pour tomato juice into a saucepan.
3. Add celery leaves, onion, sugar, salt and bay leaf to tomato juice.
4. Simmer, uncovered 10 min. stirring occasionally.
5. Meanwhile, pour water into a small bowl.
6. Sprinkle gelatin evenly over water.
7. Let stand until softened.
8. Lightly oil the mold with salad or cooking oil (not olive oil); set aside to drain.
9. Remove tomato juice mixture from heat and strain into a large bowl. Immediately add the softened gelatin to hot tomato juice mixture and stir until gelatin is completely dissolved.
10. Add cider vinegar and stir well.
11. Pour tomato-juice mixture into the prepared mold. Cool; chill in refrigerator until firm.
12. Unmold onto chilled serving plate.

6 to 8 servings

Individual Tomato Aspic Molds: Follow recipe for Tomato Aspic. Use eight ½-cup individual molds instead of the 1-qt. mold.

Cottage Cheese in Tomato Aspic: Follow recipe for Tomato Aspic. After adding vinegar to tomato juice mixture, chill until mixture is slightly thicker than consistency of thick, unbeaten egg white. Meanwhile, mix together 1 cup **cream-style cottage cheese,** 2 tablespoons grated **onion,** ⅛ teaspoon **pepper.** When gelatin mixture is of desired consistency, blend in the cottage cheese mixture. Turn into the prepared mold and chill in refrigerator until firm.

Beet Salad Mold

1 **16-oz. can diced beets (about 2 cups, drained)**
1 **3-oz. pkg. lemon-flavored gelatin**
1 **cup very hot water**
3 **tablespoons cider vinegar**
½ **teaspoon salt**
½ **cup diced celery**
2 **tablespoons grated onion**
1 **tablespoon prepared horse-radish**

1. Set out a 1-qt. mold.
2. Drain diced beets, reserving liquid.
3. Empty gelatin into a bowl.
4. Add water to bowl and stir until gelatin is completely dissolved.
5. Stir vinegar and salt into the reserved beet liquid.
6. Cool; chill until gelatin mixture is slightly thicker than consistency of thick, unbeaten egg white.
7. Meanwhile, lightly oil the mold with salad or cooking oil (not olive oil); set aside to drain.
8. Dice enough celery to yield ½ cup.
9. When gelatin mixture is of desired consistency, mix in the diced beets, celery, onion and horse-radish.
10. Turn into the prepared mold and chill in refrigerator until firm.
11. Unmold onto chilled serving plate.

6 to 8 servings

Creamy Beet Salad Mold: Follow recipe for Beet Salad Mold. Decrease vinegar to 1 tablespoon and omit horse-radish. Blend ½ cup **thick sour cream** into gelatin mixture with the diced beets.

Beet and Cucumber Salad: Follow recipe for Beet Salad Mold. Decrease beets to 1 cup and vinegar to 2 tablespoons. Omit celery. Rinse and pare 1 small **cucumber.** Remove and discard seeds. Dice enough of the cucumber to yield ¾ cup diced cucumber. Mix in the cucumber with the diced beets.

Perfection Salad Surprise

½ cup cold water
1 env. unflavored gelatin
¾ cup water
3 tablespoons sugar
2 tablespoons cider vinegar
1 tablespoon lemon juice
½ teaspoon salt
1 cup shredded cabbage
½ cup finely chopped celery
⅓ cup shredded carrot
¼ cup sliced stuffed olives
¼ cup chopped sweet pickle
3 tablespoons chopped green pepper
½ cup cold water
1 env. unflavored gelatin
1 cup cream-style cottage cheese
⅔ cup milk or cream
⅔ cup mayonnaise
1 tablespoon lemon juice
1 tablespoon minced chives
¼ teaspoon salt
⅛ teaspoon paprika

1. Set out a 1½-qt. mold.
2. For Cabbage Layer—Pour ½ cup cold water into a small cup or custard cup.
3. Sprinkle gelatin evenly over water.
4. Let stand until softened.
5. Heat ¾ cup water until very hot.
6. Remove from heat and immediately add softened gelatin, stirring until gelatin is completely dissolved. Stir in sugar, cider vinegar, lemon juice and ½ teaspoon salt.
7. Cool; chill until mixture is slightly thicker than consistency of thick, unbeaten egg white.
8. Meanwhile, lightly oil the mold with salad or cooking oil (not olive oil); set aside to drain.
9. Prepare, and mix together cabbage, celery, carrot, olives, pickle and green pepper in a bowl.
10. When gelatin mixture is of desired consistency, mix in the vegetables. Turn into the prepared mold. Chill in refrigerator until mixture is partially set.
11. For Cottage Cheese Layer—Meanwhile, pour ½ cup cold water into a small cup or custard cup.
12. Sprinkle unflavored gelatin evenly over water.
13. Let stand until softened.
14. Dissolve gelatin completely by placing cup over very hot water. Stir gelatin and blend into a mixture of cottage cheese, milk or cream, mayonnaise, lemon juice, chives, salt and paprika.
15. Chill until mixture begins to gel (gets slightly thicker).
16. When first layer in mold is partially set, immediately spoon the cottage cheese mixture into the mold. (Both layers should be of almost the same consistency when combined to avoid separation when unmolded). Chill in refrigerator until firm.
17. Unmold onto chilled serving plate.

8 to 10 servings

Perfection Salad: Follow recipe for Perfection Salad Surprise. For Cabbage Layer only. Use a 1-qt. mold. Increase cabbage to 1½ cups, celery to ¾ cup and carrot to ½ cup. Chill until firm and unmold.

Jellied Pineapple-Grape Salad: Follow recipe for Perfection Salad Surprise. For Cabbage Layer only. Use a 1-qt. mold. Omit pickle and olives. Mix in ½ cup drained **crushed pineapple** and ½ cup seeded and halved **Tokay grapes.** Chill until firm and unmold.

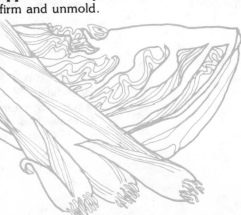

Deviled Egg Salad

6	eggs
½	cup cold water
1	env. unflavored gelatin
3	oz. (1 pkg.) cream cheese, softened
½	cup mayonnaise
¼	cup ketchup
2	tablespoons cider vinegar
3	drops Tabasco
¼	cup finely chopped green pepper
¼	cup finely chopped celery
2	tablespoons finely chopped pimiento
1	tablespoon finely chopped parsley
1	teaspoon grated onion
1	teaspoon salt

1. Hard-cook eggs and chill.
2. Meanwhile, lightly oil six ½-cup individual molds with salad or cooking oil (not olive oil); set aside to drain.
3. Pour water into a small cup or custard cup.
4. Sprinkle gelatin evenly over water.
5. Let stand until softened.
6. Meanwhile, beat together cream cheese, mayonnaise, ketchup, vinegar and Tabasco until fluffy.
7. Dissolve gelatin completely by placing cup over very hot water. Stir it and add gradually to the cream cheese mixture.
8. Chop the hard-cooked eggs. Add to the cream cheese mixture with green pepper, celery, pimiento, parsley, onion and salt.
9. Mix thoroughly. Turn into the prepared molds and chill in refrigerator until firm.
10. Unmold onto chilled serving plates. If desired, serve with slices of cold **ham;** garnish with **water cress.**

6 servings

Egg Salad: Follow recipe for Deviled Egg Salad. Omit molds. Reserve 1 hard-cooked egg for garnish. Decrease mayonnaise to ¼ cup and ketchup to 2 tablespoons. Omit gelatin, cold water, vinegar and tabasco. Spoon onto **Bibb lettuce leaves** and top each serving with a slice of egg. Or garnish each serving generously with minced **parsley** before topping with egg slice.

Chicken Salad Sensation

1	3-oz. pkg. lemon-flavored gelatin
1	cup very hot water
1	cup ginger ale
1	tablespoon lemon juice
1½	cups mayonnaise
2	cups cubed cooked chicken (see Stewed Chicken, page 40)
⅔	cup halved and seeded Tokay grapes
½	cup (about 3 oz.) chopped blanched almonds
⅓	cup chopped celery
⅓	cup chopped green pepper

1. Set out a 1½-qt. mold.
2. Empty gelatin into a bowl.
3. Add and stir water until gelatin is completely dissolved.
4. Blend in ginger ale and lemon juice.
5. Put mayonnaise into a large bowl.
6. Add the gelatin mixture gradually, stirring constantly until blended. Chill until mixture begins to gel (gets slightly thicker).
7. Lightly oil the mold with salad or cooking oil (not olive oil); set aside.
8. Prepare chicken, grapes, almonds, celery and green pepper and set aside.
9. When gelatin mixture is of desired consistency, stir in the chicken, grapes, almonds, celery and green pepper. Turn into the prepared mold and chill in refrigerator until firm.
10. Unmold onto chilled serving plate.

8 to 10 servings

Chicken-Tomato Aspic Ring

2 cups tomato juice
3 tablespoons chopped onion
½ teaspoon salt
⅛ teaspoon pepper
2 or 3 drops Tabasco
1 3-oz. pkg. lemon-flavored gelatin
⅔ cup packaged pre-cooked rice
1 cup chopped cooked chicken (see Stewed Chicken, page 40)
½ cup chopped celery
¼ cup chopped stuffed olives
¼ cup cold water
1 env. unflavored gelatin
1 cup mayonnaise
½ cup cream
½ teaspoon salt
¼ teaspoon paprika
⅛ teaspoon pepper
⅛ teaspoon crushed dried tarragon leaves

1. Lightly oil a 1½-qt. ring mold with salad or cooking oil (not olive oil); set aside to drain.
2. For Tomato Aspic Layer—Pour tomato juice into a saucepan.
3. Add to tomato juice onion, ½ teaspoon salt, 1/8 teaspoon pepper and tabasco.
4. Simmer, uncovered, 10 min.
5. Meanwhile, empty gelatin into a bowl.
6. Remove tomato juice mixture from heat. Strain into the bowl with gelatin and stir until gelatin is completely dissolved.
7. Pour into the prepared mold. Cool; chill in refrigerator until partially set.
8. For Chicken-Rice Layer—Meanwhile, cook rice according to directions on package.
9. Turn rice into a large bowl; let stand until cooled.
10. Chop and set aside enough cooked chicken to yield 1 cup.
11. Prepare celery and olives.
12. Pour water into a small cup or custard cup.
13. Sprinkle 1 env. unflavored gelatin evenly over water.
14. Let stand until softened. Dissolve completely by placing cup over very hot water. Stir gelatin and blend into a mixture of mayonnaise, cream, ½ teaspoon salt, paprika, 1/8 teaspoon pepper and tarragon leaves.
15. Add the chopped chicken, celery, olives and the mayonnaise mixture to bowl containing cooled rice; mix thoroughly.
16. When first layer in mold is partially set, immediately spoon the chicken-rice mixture into the mold. (Both layers should be of almost the same consistency when combined to avoid separation when unmolded). Chill in refrigerator until firm.
17. Unmold onto chilled serving plate.

8 to 10 servings

Turkey-Tomato Aspic Ring: Follow recipe for Chicken-Tomato Aspic Ring. Substitute cooked **turkey** for the chicken.

Avocado-Tomato Aspic Ring: Follow recipe for Chicken-Tomato Aspic Ring. For Tomato Aspic only; use a 1-qt. mold. Add 3 tablespoons chopped **celery leaves,** 1 tablespoon **sugar** and ½ **bay leaf** to tomato juice mixture before heating. Substitute **strawberry-flavored gelatin** for lemon-flavored gelatin and add 1 tablespoon **lemon juice.** Cool; chill until gelatin mixture is slightly thicker than consistency of thick, unbeaten egg white. Meanwhile, prepare 1½ cups diced **avocado.** When gelatin mixture is of desired consistency mix, in the diced avocado. Turn into the prepared mold and chill in refrigerator until firm.

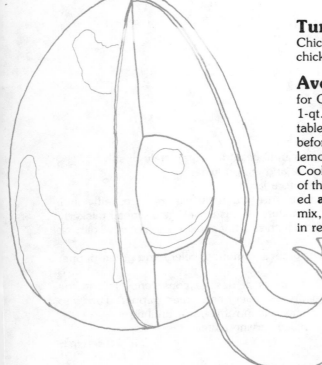

Lime and Cottage Cheese Loaf

1	3-oz. pkg. lime-flavored gelatin
1	cup very hot water
1	medium-size cucumber
1	cup cream-style cottage cheese
½	cup mayonnaise
⅓	cup sliced ripe olives
2	teaspoons grated onion
½	teaspoon salt
⅛	teaspoon white pepper
3	oz. (1 pkg.) cream cheese, softened
1	tablespoon salad dressing
¾	teaspoon grated onion
⅛	teaspoon salt

1. Set out a 9½x5¼x2¾-in. loaf pan.
2. Empty gelatin into a bowl.
3. Add and stir water until gelatin is completely dissolved.
4. Cool; chill until mixture is slightly thicker than consistency of thick, unbeaten egg white.
5. Lightly oil the pan with salad or cooking oil (not olive oil); set aside to drain.
6. Rinse cucumber and pare.
7. Cut into halves lengthwise; remove and discard seeds. Dice the cucumber (enough to yield 1 cup, diced). Mix with cottage cheese, mayonnaise, olives, onion and a mixture of ½ teaspoon salt and white pepper.
8. When gelatin mixture is of desired consistency, blend in the cottage cheese mixture. Turn into the prepared pan and chill in refrigerator until firm.
9. Mix together cream cheese, salad dressing, onion and 1/8 teaspoon salt and set in refrigerator to chill and to allow flavors to blend.
10. To serve, unmold onto a chilled serving plate. Spread cream cheese mixture over top of mold.

About 8 servings

Lime and Pineapple Mold: Follow recipe for Lime and Cottage Cheese Loaf. Use a 1-qt. mold. Drain contents of 1 20 oz. can **crushed pineapple** and set aside. Omit cucumber, mayonnaise, olives, onion, salt and pepper. When gelatin mixture is of desired consistency, stir in the drained crushed pineapple, ½ cup diced **celery** and ½ cup chopped **walnuts** and the cottage cheese. Omit cream cheese topping.

Lime-Mango Salad: Follow recipe for Lime and Cottage Cheese Loaf. Chill a bowl and rotary beater in refrigerator. Chill ½ cup **undiluted evaporated milk** in freezing compartment of refrigerator until icy cold. Use a 1½-qt. mold. Omit cucumber, mayonnaise, olives, onion, salt and pepper. Rinse, cut into halves, remove and discard pits, peel and dice enough mangoes to yield 2 cups diced **mango.** Toss lightly with 3 tablespoons **lime juice.** When gelatin mixture is of desired consistency, stir in mango with cottage cheese. Using chilled bowl and beater, beat evaporated milk until very stiff; fold into the gelatin mixture. Omit cream cheese topping.

Horse-radish Salad Mold: Follow recipe for Lime and Cottage Cheese Loaf. Use an 8x8x2-in. pan. Prepare double recipe, but use ⅔ cup mayonnaise and 2 tablespoons grated onion. Omit the cucumber and olives. Add 1 cup cold water to the dissolved gelatin before cooling, and add ½ cup **prepared horse-radish** with the cottage cheese. Omit cream cheese topping.

Ham and Orange Soufflé Salad

1¼	cups diced cooked ham
¾	cup orange sections, cut
¼	cup (about 1 oz.) chopped walnuts
1	3-oz. pkg. orange-flavored gelatin
1	cup very hot water
½	cup cold water
½	cup mayonnaise
2	tablespoons cider vinegar
1	teaspoon grated onion
¼	teaspoon salt
⅛	teaspoon pepper

1. Set out a 1-qt. mold. Set a bowl in refrigerator to chill.
2. Prepare ham, orange sections and walnuts and set aside.
3. Empty gelatin into a bowl.
4. Add and stir 1 cup very hot water until gelatin is completely dissolved.
5. Add cold water, mayonnaise, vinegar, onion, salt and pepper and beat with rotary beater until smooth.
6. Pour mixture into a refrigerator tray and put into freezing compartment of refrigerator (set for normal operating temperature) 15 to 20 min., or until edges are firm about 1 in. from sides of tray, but center is still soft.
7. Lightly oil the mold with salad or cooking oil (not olive oil); set aside to drain.
8. When gelatin mixture is of desired consistency, turn into the chilled bowl and beat with rotary beater just until fluffy. Mix in the ham, orange pieces and walnuts. Turn mixture into prepared mold and chill in refrigerator (not in the freezing compartment) 30 to 60 min., or until firm.
9. Unmold; garnish.

4 to 6 servings

Colorful Soufflé Salad: Follow recipe for Ham and Orange Soufflé Salad. Substitute **lemon-flavored gelatin.** Omit vinegar, ham, orange, walnuts and pepper. Blend 3 or 4 drops **Tabasco** into the mayonnaise mixture. Mix into the whipped gelatin 1 cup (about ¼ lb.) shredded sharp **Cheddar cheese,** 2 **hard-cooked eggs,** chopped, ⅓ cup diced **celery,** 2 tablespoons diced **pimiento** and 2 tablespoons diced **green pepper.**

Molded Cottage Cheese and Olive Salad

1	cup cold water
2	env. unflavored gelatin
1¼	cups (10½- to 11-oz. can) condensed tomato soup
1	cup chopped ripe olives
½	cup chopped celery
⅓	cup chopped green pepper
2	tablespoons chopped pimiento
1	tablespoon minced onion
2	cups cream-style cottage cheese
⅓	cup mayonnaise
2	tablespoons lemon juice
2	teaspoons Worcestershire sauce
	Few grains pepper
	Whole ripe olives
	Bits of pimiento
	Green pepper strips

1. Set out an 8½x4½x2½-in. loaf pan.
2. Pour water into a small bowl.
3. Sprinkle gelatin evenly over water.
4. Let stand until softened.
5. Meanwhile, heat tomato soup until very hot.
6. Remove from heat, add softened gelatin and stir until gelatin is completely dissolved. Cool; chill until mixture begins to gel (gets slightly thicker).
7. Lightly oil the pan with salad or cooking oil (not olive oil); set aside to drain.
8. Prepare olives, celery, green pepper, chopped pimiento and onion. Combine and set aside.
9. Force cottage cheese through a sieve into a bowl.
10. Blend with the cheese mayonnaise, lemon juice, Worcestershire sauce and a few grains pepper.
11. When gelatin mixture is of desired consistency, blend in the cheese mixture. Stir in the vegetables. Turn into the prepared pan and chill in refrigerator until firm.
12. Unmold onto chilled serving plate. Garnish with olives, pimiento and pepper strips.
13. Arrange small lettuce leaves and additional whole ripe olives around salad loaf.

About 8 servings

Two-Layer Chicken and Cranberry Salad

½ cup cold water
1 env. unflavored gelatin
4 cups (2 16-oz. cans) whole cranberry sauce
1 cup (8¾-oz. can) crushed pineapple
⅓ cup (about 1½ oz.) chopped walnuts
2 cups cubed cooked chicken (see Stewed Chicken, page 40)
¾ cup finely chopped celery
3 tablespoons chopped parsley
½ cup cold water
1 env. unflavored gelatin
1 cup mayonnaise
½ cup undiluted evaporated milk
½ teaspoon salt

1. Lightly oil a 3-qt. mold with salad or cooking oil (not olive oil); set aside to drain.
2. For Cranberry Layer—Pour ½ cup cold water into a small cup or custard cup.
3. Sprinkle 1 env. unflavored gelatin evenly over water.
4. Let stand until softened.
5. Mix together cranberry sauce, pineapple and walnuts in a large bowl.
6. Dissolve gelatin completely by placing cup over very hot water. Stir it and blend into cranberry mixture. Turn into the prepared mold. Chill in refrigerator until partially set.
7. For Chicken Layer—Prepare chicken, celery and parsley.
8. Pour ½ cup cold water into a small cup or custard cup.
9. Sprinkle 1 env. unflavored gelatin evenly over water.
10. Let stand until softened.
11. Mix together mayonnaise, evaporated milk and salt in a bowl.
12. Dissolve gelatin completely by placing cup over very hot water. Stir it and blend into mayonnaise mixture. Stir in the chicken, celery, and parsley.
13. When first layer in mold is partially set, immediately spoon the chicken layer into the mold. (Both layers should be of almost the same consistency when combined to avoid separation when unmolded). Chill in refrigerator until firm.
14. Unmold onto chilled serving plate, Garnish with **water cress.**

About 12 servings

Note: A 9½x5¼x2¾-in. loaf pan may be substitute for the 3-qt. mold.

Ham Mousse

1 lb. chopped ham
2 small chopped cucumbers
1 bunch chopped dill
1 cup heavy cream
2½ teaspoons prepared mustard
2 teaspoons unflavored gelatin
6 tablespoons cold water
2 tomatoes
1 frozen turkey roll (1 lb.)
1 can white sparagus with tips (1 lb.)
1 package frozen peas (cooked according to directions)
1 can creamed mushrooms (8 oz.)

1. Mix the chopped ham, cucumber and dill.
2. Beat the cream to a light foam and season with the mustard.
3. Melt the gelatin in ¼ cup cold water in a double boiler.
4. Stir the melted gelatin and the chopped ham into the cream. Pour into a water-rinsed ring mold, and place the mousse in the refrigerator to set.
5. Dip the tomatoes in hot water, remove the skin and cut them in halves.
6. Carve the turkey roll in even slices. Place the ham mousse in the middle of a large round dish. If the ring mold is dipped in hot water for a moment it will slide out easily. Put the asparagus in the middle of the mousse and arrange turkey slices in groups around the mousse. Surround with tomatoes and peas. Distribute the creamed mushrooms on the turkey slices.

Serves 8 to 10

Avocado Delight

1	cup cold water
2	env. unflavored gelatin
1/2	cup very hot water
1 1/2	teaspoons sugar
1	teaspoon salt
	Few grains pepper
1	large ripe avocado
1	teaspoon grated onion
1/2	teaspoon prepared horse-radish
1/2	teaspoon lemon juice
1/4	teaspoon grated lemon peel
1	cup diced cooked chicken (see Stewed Chicken, page 40)
1	cup diced cooked ham
1/4	cup (about 1 oz.) chopped pecans
1	cup thick sour cream
1/4	cup mayonnaise
1/2	cup chilled whipping cream

1. Set out a 1½-qt. ring mold. Set a bowl and rotary beater in refrigerator to chill.
2. Pour 1 cup cold water into a small bowl.
3. Sprinkle 2 env. unflavored gelatin evenly over water.
4. Let stand until softened.
5. Add and stir ½ cup very hot water until gelatin is completely dissolved.
6. Blend in thoroughly sugar, salt and pepper.
7. Prepare avocado and cut into pieces.
8. Force avocado through a sieve or food mill into a mixing bowl. Mix in onion, horse-radish, juice and lemon peel.
9. Blend in the gelatin mixture. Chill until mixture begins to gel (gets slightly thicker). Lightly oil the mold with salad or cooking oil (not olive oil); set aside to drain.
10. Prepare chicken, ham, and chopped pecans.
11. When gelatin mixture is of desired consistency, blend in sour cream and mayonnaise.
12. Mix in the chicken, ham and pecans.
13. Using the chilled bowl and beater, beat whipping cream until cream is of medium consistency (piles softly).
14. Fold whipped cream into gelatin mixture. Turn into the prepared mold and chill in refrigerator until firm.
15. Unmold onto a chilled serving plate. Garnish with **water cress.**

8 to 10 servings

Tuna Salad Mold

1/2	cup cold water
1/2	cup cold chicken broth
2	env. unflavored gelatin
2	oz. Cheddar cheese (about 1/2 cup, grated)
1/2	cup very hot quick chicken broth (page 9)
1	cup mayonnaise
2	tablespoons lemon juice
1	tablespoon minced onion
1/2	teaspoon Worcestershire sauce
1/8	teaspoon salt
1/8	teaspoon cayenne pepper
1/2	cup (about 3 oz.) slivered and toasted blanched almonds
1/2	cup sliced stuffed olives
1	7-oz. can tuna (about 1 cup, flaked)

1. Set out a 1-qt. mold (fish-shape, if desired).
2. Pour water and ½ cup cold chicken broth into a small bowl.
3. Sprinkle gelatin evenly over water.
4. Let stand until softened.
5. Grate Cheddar cheese and set aside.
6. Prepare ½ cup very hot quick chicken broth.
7. Stir in softened gelatin until completely dissolved.
8. Put mayonnaise into a large bowl.
9. Add the gelatin mixture gradually, stirring constantly. Blend in the grated cheese and lemon juice, onion, Worcestershire sauce and a mixture of salt and pepper.
10. Chill until mixture begins to gel (gets slightly thicket).
11. Lightly oil the mold with salad or cooking oil (not olive oil); set aside to drain.
12. Prepare almonds and olives and set aside.
13. Drain and flake contents of can tuna.
14. When gelatin mixture is of desired consistency, stir in the almonds, olives and tuna (reserve one olive slice if using a fish-shape mold). Turn into the prepared mold and chill in refrigerator until firm.
15. Unmold onto chilled platter. If mold is fish-shape, place reserved olive slice on head of fish for the eye. Garnish with crisp **lettuce leaves.**

6 to 8 servings

Salad Dressings

Cooked Salad Dressing

¼ cup sugar
1 tablespoon all-purpose flour
½ teaspoon dry mustard
½ teaspoon salt
⅛ teaspoon pepper
1 cup water
¼ cup cider vinegar
4 egg yolks, slightly beaten
2 tablespoons butter

1. Mix sugar, flour, dry mustard, salt and pepper thoroughly in the top of a double boiler.
2. Blend water in gradually.
3. Set over direct heat. Stirring gently and constantly, bring mixture to boiling. Cook 1 to 2 min. longer. Add and stir in vinegar.
4. Vigorously stir about 3 tablespoons of the hot mixture into egg yolks.
5. Immediately blend into mixture in top of double boiler. Place over simmering water and cook 3 to 5 min., stirring slowly to keep mixture cooking evenly. Remove from heat and stir in butter.
6. Cool; store in covered container in refrigerator. Before using, thin to desired consistency with cream, fruit juice or cider vinegar.

About 1½ cups salad dressing

Dressing for Overnight Fruit Salad: Follow recipe for Cooked Salad Dressing. Use 2 tablespoons **sugar**, 2 tablespoons **cider vinegar** and 2 tablespoons **pineapple syrup.** Bring mixture only to boiling. Substitute 3 **egg yolks** and 1 tablespoon **butter.** When dressing is cooled, beat 1 cup chilled **whipping cream** until it is of medium consistency (piles softly). Fold the cooled dressing into the whipped cream.

About 2 cups dressing

Tangy Salad Dressing

2	egg yolks
2	tablespoons cider vinegar
2	tablespoons lemon juice
1	tablespoon sugar
1	teaspoon salt
½	teaspoon dry mustard
	Few grains pepper
¾	cup salad oil
3	tablespoons butter or margarine
¼	cup all-purpose flour
1	cup water

1. Beat together in a bowl egg yolks, vinegar, lemon juice, sugar, salt, dry mustard, cayenne pepper and salad oil.
2. Set aside.
3. Heat butter or margarine in a saucepan until melted.
4. Stir in and cook flour mixing well, until bubbly.
5. Remove from heat and gradually add water stirring constantly.
6. Return to heat and cook until boiling, stirring constantly. Cook and stir about 3 min. longer.
7. Gradually spoon cooked mixture into egg mixture, beating with a rotary beater until thick and smooth. Cool. Store in covered container in refrigerator.
8. If desired, thin to desired consistency with cream before using.

About 2 cups dressing

Low-Calorie Salad Dressing

2	eggs
½	cup reconstituted nonfat dry milk (use double amount of milk solids)
½	teaspoon paprika
½	teaspoon dry mustard
2	drops Tabasco
¼	cup cider vinegar

1. Beat eggs slightly in top of a double boiler.
2. Blend in milk, paprika, dry mustard and Tabasco.
3. Place over simmering water. Add gradually, stirring in cider vinegar.
4. Cook over simmering water, stirring constantly, until mixture thickens (about 10 min.).
5. Remove from heat. Cool. Store in covered container in refrigerator.

About 1 cup dressing

Note: For a less sharp dressing, decrease vinegar to 2 tablespoons and increase milk to ½ cup plus 2 tablespoons.

Flavorful Salad Dressing: Follow recipe for Low-Calorie Salad Dressing. Blend 2 tablespoons grated **onion** into mixture in top of double boiler. Decrease cider vinegar to 2 tablespoons. Blend into cooled dressing ¼ cup **ketchup** or **chili sauce.**

Cooked Sour-Cream Dressing

⅔	cup sugar
2	tablespoons all-purpose flour
½	teaspoon salt
½	cup cider vinegar or lemon juice
3	eggs, slightly beaten
1	cup thick sour cream
2	teaspoons prepared mustard

1. Mix sugar, flour and salt thoroughly in the top of a double boiler.
2. Add vinegar or lemon juice gradually, blending until smooth.
3. Set over direct heat. Stirring gently and constantly, bring mixture to boiling. Cook 1 or 2 min. longer. Remove from heat and vigorously stir about 3 tablespoons of the hot mixture into eggs.
4. Immediately blend into mixture in top of the double boiler. Place over simmering water and cook 3 to 5 min., stirring slowly to keep mixture cooking evenly. Remove from heat and add sour cream and prepared mustard very gradually, stirring until well blended.
5. Cool. Store in covered container in refrigerator.
6. If desired, thin with cream before using.

About 2½ cups dressing

Hot Sour Cream Dressing for Greens

4	slices bacon, cut into ¼-in. pieces
¼	cup chopped onion
2	tablespoons sugar
2	teaspoons all-purpose flour
¾	teaspoon salt
1	cup thick sour cream
2	tablespoons cider vinegar

1. Panbroil bacon, reserving fat.
2. Return ¼ cup of the fat to skillet and add onion.
3. Cook until the onion is tender, moving and turning occasionally with a spoon. Blend in sugar, flour and salt.
4. Heat until mixture bubbles. Remove from heat. Stirring vigorously, add sour cream in very small amounts.
5. Cook over medium heat, stirring constantly, until slightly thicker; cook 2 or 3 min. longer, keeping the sauce moving constantly. *Do not boil.*
6. Remove from heat. Mix in the bacon and cider vinegar.
7. Pour hot dressing over crisp salad greens (leaf lettuce, curly endive, raw spinach, or a mixture of such greens). Toss lightly and serve at once.

About 1¼ cups dressing

Mayonnaise

2	egg yolks
1	tablespoon cider vinegar
½	teaspoon dry mustard
½	teaspoon salt
¼	teaspoon sugar
⅛	teaspoon white pepper
	Few grains cayenne pepper
1	cup salad oil
1	tablespoon lemon juice

1. Put into a small bowl egg yolks, vinegar, dry mustard, salt, sugar, white pepper and cayenne pepper and beat with a rotary beater until well blended.
2. Measure salad oil.
3. Add oil, 1 teaspoon at a time at first, beating vigorously after each addition. Gradually increase amounts added until one half of the salad oil has been used.
4. Alternately beat in small amounts of remaining salad oil and lemon juice (a few drops at a time). (If mayonnaise separates because oil has been added too rapidly, beat it slowly and thoroughly into 1 egg yolk, 1 tablespoon cold water, small quantity of vinegar or small portion of good mayonnaise.) Store in covered container in refrigerator.

About 1½ cups Mayonnaise

Elegant Mayonnaise: Follow recipe for Mayonnaise. Blend into 1 cup chilled Mayonnaise 1 teaspoon **lemon juice,** 1 teaspoon **curry powder** and a few grains of **salt.** Using a chilled bowl and beater, beat ⅓ cup chilled **whipping cream** until cream is of medium consistency (piles softly). With final few strokes, beat or blend in 2 tablespoons plus 1 teaspoon **sifted confectioners' sugar.** Fold whipped cream into Mayonnaise mixture.

Thousand Island Dressing: Follow recipe for Mayonnaise. Mix into ½ cup Mayonnaise 1 or 2 **hard-cooked eggs,** sieved or finely chopped, 2 tablespoons **chili sauce,** 2 tablespoons finely chopped **scallions** (with tops), 2 tablespoons chopped **green olives** and ½ teaspoon **paprika.**

Russian Dressing: Follow recipe for Mayonnaise. Blend into ½ cup Mayonnaise 3 tablespoons **chili sauce,** 1 tablespoon minced **onion** and ½ teaspoon **prepared horseradish.**

Sour Cream Mayonnaise: Blend into ½ cup Mayonnaise ½ cup **thick sour cream,** 2 teaspoons **cider vinegar,** 1 teaspoon **sugar** and ½ teaspoon **dry mustard.**

French Dressing

¾ cup salad oil or olive oil
¼ cup lemon juice or cider
    vinegar
1 tablespoon sugar
¾ teaspoon salt
¼ teaspoon paprika
¼ teaspoon dry mustard
¼ teaspoon pepper

1. Combine in a screw-top jar salad oil or olive oil, lemon juice or cider vinegar, sugar, salt, paprika, dry mustard and pepper.
2. Cover jar tightly and shake vigorously to blend well. Store in covered container in refrigerator.
3. Shake well before using.

About 1 cup dressing

Anchovy French Dressing: Follow recipe for French Dressing. Use lemon juice. Omit salt and add 4 minced **anchovy fillets.** Shake well.

Lorenzo French Dressing: Follow recipe for French Dressing. Add ¼ cup finely chopped **water cress** and 2 tablespoons **chili sauce.** Shake well.

Olive French Dressing: Follow recipe for French Dressing. Add ½ cup chopped **stuffed olives** and shake well.

Tangy French Dressing: Follow recipe for French Dressing. Add 3 to 4 tablespoons **prepared horse-radish** and shake well.

Curried French Dressing: Follow recipe for French Dressing. Add ¼ teaspoon **curry powder** and shake well.

Fruit Juice French Dressing: Follow recipe for French Dressing. Substitute **orange** or **pineapple juice** for the lemon juice or vinegar, or use 2 tablespoons of each fruit juice.

Creamy French Dressing: Follow recipe for French Dressing. Add ¼ cup **thick sour cream** and blend well.

Garlic French Dressing: Cut into halves 1 clove **garlic;** add to completed dressing. Chill dressing about 12 hours before using to allow flavors to blend. Remove garlic before serving or when flavor of dressing is sufficiently strong.

Roquefort French Dressing: Follow recipe for French Dressing. Blend together until smooth 3 oz. (about ¾ cup) crumbled **Roquefort cheese** and 2 teaspoons **water.** Add dressing slowly to cheese, blending after each addition.

Honey-Lime French Dressing: Follow recipe for French Dressing. Substitute **lime juice** for the lemon juice or vinegar. Blend in ½ cup **honey** and ¼ teaspoon grated **lime peel.**

Vinaigrette French Dressing: Follow recipe for French Dressing. Add 2 tablespoons finely chopped **dill pickle,** 2 tablespoons chopped **chives,** and 1 **hard-cooked egg** chopped. Shake well.

Italian Dressing: Follow recipe for French Dressing. Use olive oil. Omit lemon juice or vinegar and add 6 tablespoons **wine vinegar.** Reduce salt to ½ teaspoon. Omit sugar, paprika and dry mustard. Shake well.

Tomato Soup French Dressing: Follow recipe for French Dressing. Add ⅔ cup (about one-half 10½-to 11-oz. can) **condensed tomato soup,** 1 tablespoon chopped **onion** and ½ teaspoon **marjoram.** Shake well.

Honey French Dressing: Follow recipe for French Dressing. Use lemon juice. Blend in ½ cup **honey** and ¼ teaspoon grated **lemon peel.** For added flavor, add ½ teaspoon **celery seed** and shake well.

Chiffonade French Dressing: Follow recipe for French Dressing. Add 1 **hard-cooked egg,** chopped, 2 tablespoons finely chopped **ripe olives,** and 4 teaspoons finely chopped **parsley.** Shake well.

Tarragon French Dressing: Follow recipe for French Dressing. Use olive oil. Substitute **tarragon vinegar** for lemon juice or cider vinegar. Decrease sugar to 1 teaspoon. Add 1 clove **garlic,** cut into halves, ¼ teaspoon **Worcestershire sauce** and ⅛ teaspoon **thyme.** Shake well.

Low-Calorie French Dressing

¾ **cup water**
2 **teaspoons cornstarch**
¼ **cup lemon juice**
¼ **teaspoon non-caloric sweetening solution; or 2 non-caloric sweetening tablets, crushed and dissolved in the lemon juice before adding**
¼ **cup ketchup**
2 **tablespoons salad oil**
1 **teaspoon Worcestershire sauce**
¾ **teaspoon salt**
¼ **teaspoon paprika**
¼ **teaspoon pepper**
¼ **teaspoon dry mustard**

1. Blend together water and cornstarch in a saucepan.
2. Bring to boiling over high heat. Reduce heat and cook 5 min., or until mixture is thick and clear. Remove from heat and set aside to cool.
3. When cool add lemon juice, non-caloric sweetening solution, ketchup, salad oil, Worcestershire sauce, salt, paprika, pepper and dry mustard.
4. Beat with a rotary beater until smooth and well blended. Store in covered container in refrigerator.
5. Shake well before using.

About 1¼ cups dressing

Blender Mayonnaise

1   egg, unbeaten
2   tablespoons cider vinegar
     or lemon juice
¼   teaspoon salt
¼   teaspoon sugar
¼   teaspoon dry mustard
¼   teaspoon paprika
2   or 3 drops Tabasco
½   to ¾ cup salad oil

1. Put into blender container in order egg, cider vinegar or lemon juice, salt, sugar, dry mustard, paprika and Tabasco.
2. Cover and blend thoroughly. Continue blending while pouring salad oil very slowly into center of ingredients.
3. Add oil just until it begins to layer on surface; Mayonnaise then will be proper consistency. (If Mayonnaise separates because oil is added too rapidly, beat mixture slowly and thoroughly into 1 egg yolk, 1 tablespoon cold water, small quantity of vinegar or small portion of good Mayonnaise.)
4. Store in covered container in refrigerator.

About 1 cup Mayonnaise

Blender Russian Dressing: Follow recipe for Blender Mayonnaise. Put ¼ **onion,** ⅓ cup **chili sauce** and 1 teaspoon **prepared horse-radish** into blender container with Mayonnaise. Blend until ingredients are thoroughly mixed.

Blender Thousand Island Dressing: Follow recipe for Blender Mayonnaise. Add to blender container containing Mayonnaise ¼ cup **chili sauce,** ¼ cup **stuffed olives,** ¼ cup **sweet pickle relish,** 2 or 3 **green onions** (with tops), cut into pieces and ½ teaspoon **paprika.** Cover and turn on motor. Add by quaters 1 **hard-cooked egg,** peeled and quartered. Blend only until egg is chopped.

Aromatic French Dressing

⅔   cup salad oil
¼   cup lemon juice
2   tablespoons water
2   tablespoons ketchup
1   teaspoon sugar
1   teaspoon salt
1   teaspoon aromatic bitters
½   teaspoon dry mustard
½   teaspoon oregano
½   teaspoon paprika
3   drops Tabasco
    Few grains pepper
1   clove garlic
1   very small onion

1. Combine in a scew-top jar salad oil, lemon juice, water, ketchup, sugar, salt, aromatic bitters, dry mustard, oregano, paprika, Tabasco and pepper.
2. Cut garlic and onion into halves and put into the jar.
3. Cover jar tightly and shake well. Store in covered container in refrigerator. Shake well before using.

About 1 cup dressing

Note: Remove and discard garlic and onion halves before serving, or when flavor of dressing is sufficiently strong.

Extra-Special Anchovy Dressing

1   **2-oz. can anchovy fillets**
    Salad oil (enough to make
    ⅓ cup oil)
1   **clove garlic, cut into**
    halves
½   **cup undiluted evaporated**
    milk
3   **tablespoons cider vinegar**
1   **teaspoon lemon juice**
1   **teaspoon finely chopped**
    chives
½   **teaspoon salt**
⅛   **teaspoon pepper**
⅛   **teaspoon crushed dried**
    tarragon leaves

1. Drain anchovy fillets reserving oil in a 1-cup measuring cup for liquids.
2. Add salad oil to the oil.
3. Pour into a screw-top jar. Add garlic.
4. Mash the anchovy fillets and add to oil with milk, cider vinegar, lemon juice, chives, salt, pepper and tarragon leaves.
5. Cover jar tightly and shake well. Set in refrigerator about 2 hrs. to chill and to allow flavors to blend.
6. Remove the garlic halves. Store dressing in covered container in refrigerator. Beat or shake well before using.

About 1¼ cups dressing

Dressing for Vegetable Salads

½   **cup salad oil**
½   **cup undiluted evaporated**
    milk
3   **tablespoons cider vinegar**
    or lemon juice
4   **teaspoons sugar**
1¼ **teaspoons paprika**
1   **teaspoon dry mustard**
½   **teaspoon salt**
⅛   **teaspoon pepper**
1   **teaspoon grated onion**

1. Combine in a screw-top jar salad oil, evaporated milk, cider vinegar or lemon juice, sugar, paprika, dry mustard, salt, pepper and onion.
2. Cover jar tightly and shake vigorously to blend well. Store in covered container in refrigerator. Shake well before using.

About 1¼ cups dressing

Celery Seed Dressing

4½ **tablespoons cider vinegar**
½   **cup sugar**
1   **teaspoon dry mustard**
1   **teaspoon salt**
1   **teaspoon grated onion**
1   **cup salad oil**
1   **tablespoon celery seed**

1. Set out cider vinegar.
2. Mix together sugar, dry mustard and salt in a bowl.
3. Blend in 2 tablespoons of the cider vinegar and onion.
4. Add salad oil very gradually while beating constantly.
5. Beat until thick and light. Slowly beat in the remainder of the cider vinegar. Add celery seed and mix well.
6. Store in covered container in refrigerator. Shake well before using.

About 1⅔ cups dressing

Buttermilk Salad Dressing

½   **cup buttermilk**
4   **teaspoons prepared horse-radish**
1   **teaspoon sugar**
⅛   **teaspoon dry mustard**
⅛   **teaspoon salt**
    Few grains pepper

1. Blend together buttermilk, horse-radish, sugar, dry mustard, salt and pepper.
2. Chill thoroughly. Stir or shake well before using.

About ½ cup dressing

Melbourne Salad Dressing

⅔   **cup lemon juice**
¼   **cup olive oil**
¼   **cup Worcestershire sauce**
3   **tablespoons plus 1 teaspoon sugar**

1. Combine in a screw-top jar lemon juice, olive oil, Worcestershire sauce and sugar.
2. Cover jar tightly and shake vigorously to blend well. Store in covered container in refrigerator. Shake well before using. Serve icy cold.

About 1¼ cups dressing

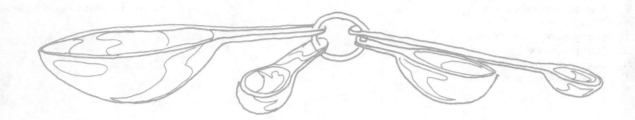

Shaker Salad Dressing

⅔   **cup sweetened condensed milk**
¼   **cup salad oil**
3   **tablespoons lemon juice or cider vinegar**
1   **tablespoons minced parsley**
1   **teaspoon prepared mustard**
½   **teaspoon salt**
    Few grains cayenne pepper

1. Combine condensed milk, salad oil, lemon juice or cider vinegar, parsley, prepared mustard, salt and cayenne pepper.
2. Cover jar tightly and shake well. Store in covered container in refrigerator. Shake well before using.

About 1 cup dressing

Favorite Salad Dressing

1   **medium-size green pepper**
1   **medium-size onion**
1/3 **cup orange juice**
1/4 **cup salad oil**
3   **tablespoons lemon juice**
2   **tablespoons cider vinegar**
2   **tablespoons sugar**
1/2 **teaspoon salt**
1/4 **teaspoon pepper**
1   **clove garlic, cut into halves**

1. Put through fine blade of food chopper green pepper and onion.
2. Combine in a screw-top jar with orange juice, salad oil, lemon juice, cider vinegar, sugar, salt, pepper and garlic.
3. Cover jar tightly and shake well. Store in covered container in refrigerator. Shake well before serving.

About 1 1/2 cups dressing

Note: Remove and discard garlic halves before serving, or when flavor of dressing is sufficiently strong.

Green Goddess Salad Dressing

1   **cup mayonnaise**
1/2 **cup thick sour cream**
3   **tablespoons tarragon vinegar**
1   **tablespoon lemon juice**
1/3 **cup finely chopped parsley**
3   **tablespoons finely chopped onion**
3   **tablespoons mashed anchovy fillets**
1   **tablespoon chopped chives**
2   **teaspoons chopped capers**
1   **clove garlic, crushed in a garlic press or minced**
1/8 **teaspoon salt**
1/8 **teaspoon pepper**

1. Blend thoroughly mayonnaise, sour cream, tarragon vinegar, lemon juice, parsley, onion and anchovy fillets, chives, capers, garlic, salt and pepper.
2. Cover bowl tightly and chill in refrigerator 3 to 4 hrs.
3. Serve on Green Goddess Salad.

About 2 1/2 cups dressing

Tarragon Salad Dressing

1/4 **cup sugar**
1/4 **cup light corn syrup**
1/4 **cup tarragon vinegar**
1 1/2 **teaspoons celery seed**
1   **teaspoon dry mustard**
1   **teaspoon salt**
1/2 **teaspoon grated onion**
     Few grains white pepper
3/4 **cup salad oil**

1. Put into a small bowl sugar, corn syrup, vinegar, celery seed, dry mustard, salt, onion and white pepper.
2. Beat with rotary beater until thoroughly mixed.
3. Add salad oil very gradually while beating constantly.
4. Continue beating until mixture is of desired consistency.
5. Chill thoroughly in covered container in refrigerator. Shake well before serving.

About 1 1/2 cups dressing

Pineapple Salad Dressing

1½ cups pineapple juice
½ cup sugar
1 tablespoon cornstarch
⅛ teaspoon salt
2 egg yolks, slightly beaten
2 egg whites
2 tablespoons sugar
2 tablespoons butter
¾ cup chilled whipping cream

1. Set out pineapple juice.
2. Sift together sugar, cornstarch and salt into top of a double boiler.
3. Stir in ½ cup of the pineapple juice. Stirring gently and constantly, bring mixture rapidly to boiling over direct heat and cook for 3 min. Place over simmering water. Vigorously stir about 3 tablespoons of the hot mixture into egg yolks.
4. Immediately blend into mixture in double boiler. Cook over simmering water 3 to 5 min. Stir slowly to keep mixture cooking evenly. Remove double boiler from heat.
5. Beat egg whites until frothy.
6. Add 2 tablespoons sugar gradually, beating well after each addition.
7. Beat until rounded peaks are formed. Gently blend into mixture in top of double boiler.
8. Heat the remaining 1 cup pineapple juice to lukewarm. Stirring constantly, gradually add to egg white mixture.
9. Cook over simmering water until thick and smooth, stirring constantly (about 10 min.). Add and stir butter until melted.
10. Remove from heat and set aside to cool. Set in refrigerator to chill.
11. Meanwhile, set a bowl and rotary beater in refrigerator to chill.
12. When pineapple mixture is chilled, using the chilled bowl and beater, beat whipping cream until cream is of medium consistency (piles softly).
13. Gently fold whipped cream into pineapple mixture.

About 4 cups dressing.

Rum-Flavored Dressing

3 tablespoons olive oil
4 teaspoons lime juice
4 teaspoons rum
2 teaspoons brown sugar
¼ teaspoon salt
  Few grains pepper

1. Combine in a screw-top jar olive oil, lime juice, rum, brown sugar, salt and pepper.
2. Cover jar tightly and shake vigorously to blend well. Store in covered container in refrigerator. Shake well before using.

About ⅓ cup dressing

Orange Fruit-Salad Dressing

½ cup orange juice
¼ cup sugar
⅛ teaspoon salt
2 egg yolks, slightly beaten
2 egg whites
2 tablespoons sugar
1 tablespoon lemon juice
1 tablespoon butter
¼ cup chilled whipping cream
½ teaspoon grated orange peel

1. Set out orange juice.
2. Combine in the top of a double boiler ¼ cup of orange juice, sugar and salt.
3. Stirring constantly, heat mixture over medium heat until sugar is dissolved and mixture simmers. Place over simmering water. Vigorously stir about 3 tablespoons of the hot mixture into egg yolks.
4. Immediately blend into mixture in top of double boiler. Place over simmering water and cook 3 to 5 min., stirring slowly to keep mixture cooking evenly. Remove from heat.
5. Beat egg whites until frothy.
6. Add 2 tablespoons of sugar gradually, beating well after each addition.
7. Beat until rounded peaks are formed. Blend beaten egg whites into orange mixture. Heat remaining orange juice to lukewarm with the lemon juice.
8. Stirring constantly, gradually add to mixture in top of double boiler. Cook over simmering water until thick and smooth (about 10 min.), stirring constantly.
9. Add and stir butter until melted.
10. Remove from heat and set aside to cool. Set in refrigerator to chill.
11. Set a bowl and rotary beater in refrigerator to chill.
12. Just before serving, using the chilled bowl and beater, beat whipping cream until cream is of medium consistency (piles softly).
13. Gently fold whipped cream into orange mixture. Spoon into serving dish. Sprinkle orange peel over top.

About 2½ cups dressing

Raspberry Fruit-Salad Dressing: Follow recipe for Orange Fruit-Salad Dressing. Substitute **raspberry fruit syrup** for the orange juice. Decrease the ¼ cup sugar to 2 tablespoons. Increase lemon juice to 3 tablespoons and omit the grated orange peel.

Apricot Fruit-Salad Dressing: Follow recipe for Orange Fruit-Salad Dressing. Omit the orange juice and add 1 cup plus 2 tablespoons **apricot nectar.** Increase lemon juice to 1½ tablespoons and omit the grated orange peel.

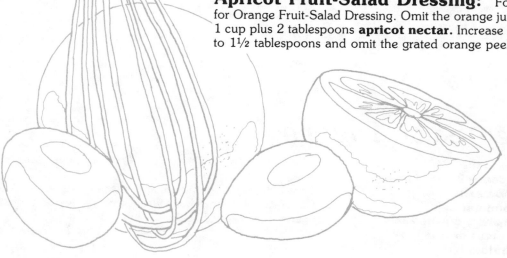

Avocado Dressing

1	medium-size ripe avocado
½	cup salad oil
2	tablespoons lemon juice
2	tablespoons minced onion
½	teaspoon salt
1	drop Tabasco
	Few grains white pepper

1. Prepare avocado and cut into pieces.
2. Force avocado pieces through a sieve or food mill into a bowl. Add salad oil very gradually while beating constantly.
3. Continue beating while adding lemon juice gradually.
4. Blend in onion, salt, Tabasco and white pepper.
5. Chill in covered container in refrigerator. Serve the same day.

About 1 cup dressing

Cooked Marshmallow Dressing

½	cup milk
½	cup cream
2	egg yolks
¼	cup sugar
2	tablespoons all-purpose flour
½	teaspoon dry mustard
¼	teaspoon salt
⅛	teaspoon white pepper
¼	cup cider vinegar
1	tablespoon plus 1 teaspoon lemon juice
2	teaspoons lime juice
16	(¼ lb.) marshmallows, cut into quarters

1. Scald milk and cream in top of double boiler over simmering water, just until thin film appears.
2. Beat egg yolks, sugar, flour, dry mustard, salt and white pepper until thick and lemon-colored.
3. Add cider vinegar, lemon juice and lime juice stirring well.
4. Vigorously stir a small amount of scalded milk and cream into egg-yolk mixture. Immediately blend into milk and cream in double boiler top. Mix in marshmallows.
5. Cook over simmering water 10 to 12 min., or until mixture thickens. Stir slowly to keep mixture cooking evenly. Cool. Store in covered container in refrigerator.

About 2 cups dressing

Chutney Salad Dressing

½	cup salad oil
3	tablespoons cider vinegar
½	teaspoon salt
¼	teaspoon nutmeg
½	clove garlic, crushed in a garlic press or minced
½	cup chutney

1. Combine in a screw-top jar salad oil, cider vinegar, salt, nutmeg and garlic.
2. Finely chop (if large pieces are present) and add chutney.
3. Cover jar tightly and shake well. Store in covered container in refrigerator. Shake well before using.

About 1¼ cups dressing

Enchanting Fruit Dressing I

½	cup water
½	cup honey
8	mint leaves
⅛	teaspoon whole cardamom seeds (contents of 3 cardamom pods), crushed
¼	teaspoon salt
½	cup sherry, Madeira, or port
1	tablespoon lemon juice

1. Put water, honey, mint leaves and cardamom seeds into a small saucepan having a tight-fitting cover.
2. Bruise the mint with the back of a spoon. Set over low heat and stir until mixed. Cover saucepan and bring rapidly to boiling. Boil gently 5 min. Remove from heat and stir in salt.
3. Set aside to cool.
4. When mixture is cool, strain it and blend in wine and lemon juice.

About 1⅓ cups dressing

Enchanting Fruit Dressing II: Follow recipe for Enchanting Fruit Dressing I. Omit fresh mint. Stir in ¼ teaspoon crushed **dried mint** with the crushed cardamom.

Fluffy Citrus Salad Dressing

3	tablespoons honey
3	teaspoons lemon, lime or orange juice
½	cup chilled whipping cream

1. Set a bowl and rotary beater in refrigerator to chill.
2. Just before serving, blend together honey, lemon, lime or orange juice.
3. Using the chilled bowl and beater, beat whipping cream until cream is of medium consistency (piles softly).
4. Beat the honey mixture into cream with final few strokes.
5. Serve with fruit salads.

About 1¼ cups dressing

Poppy Seed-Mustard Dressing

¼	cup honey
¼	cup cider vinegar
2	tablespoons prepared mustard
2	tablespoons poppy seeds
4	teaspoons grated onion
¼	teaspoon salt
⅔	cup salad oil

1. Put honey, cider vinegar, prepared mustard, poppy seeds, grated onion and salt into a small bowl.
2. Beat with rotary beater until thoroughly mixed. Add salad oil very gradually while beating constantly.
3. Continue beating until mixture is of desired consistency.
4. Chill thoroughly in covered container in refrigerator. Shake well before using.

About 1⅓ cups dressing

Snappy Salad Dressing

¼	cup butter or margarine
¼	cup ketchup
3	tablespoons cider vinegar
3	tablespoons sugar
1¼	teaspoons Worcestershire sauce
¼	teaspoon salt
¼	teaspoon paprika
¼	teaspoon Tabasco

1. Mix together in a saucepan butter or margarine, ketchup, cider vinegar, sugar, Worcestershire sauce, salt and paprika.
2. Set over direct heat. Stirring gently and constantly, bring to boiling. Remove from heat and stir in Tabasco.
3. Set aside to cool. Set in refrigerator to chill.

About ¾ cup dressing

Gourmet Salad Dressing

3	oz. Roquefort cheese (about ¾ cup, crumbled)
3	oz. (1 pkg.) cream cheese, softened
1	cup thick sour cream
⅓	cup sherry
4	teaspoons grated onion
½	teaspoon salt
¼	teaspoon paprika
1	or 2 drops Tabasco

1. Crumble Roquefort cheese into a bowl.
2. Blend in cream cheese until smooth.
3. Add and blend thoroughly sour cream, sherry, onion, salt, paprika and Tabasco.
4. Store in covered container in refrigerator.

About 2 cups dressing

Variety Salad Dressing: Follow recipe for Gourmet Salad Dressing. Omit Roquefort cheese. Blend with the cream cheese 5 oz. (1 jar) **process cheese spread with Blue cheese.** Decrease sherry to ¼ cup. Omit Tabasco sauce.

Zestful Blue Cheese Dressing

2	oz. Blue cheese (about ½ cup, crumbled)
1	cup mayonnaise
¼	cup thick sour cream
2	tablespoons cider vinegar
1	tablespoon sugar
½	clove garlic, crushed in a garlic press or minced
	Few grains salt

1. Crumble Blue cheese into a bowl.
2. Add mayonnaise, sour cream, cider vinegar, sugar, garlic and salt and blend together.
3. Beat until mixture is fluffy. Store in covered container in refrigerator.

About 1½ cups dressing

Pimiento Blue Cheese Dressing: Follow recipe for Zestful Blue Cheese Dressing. Mix in 3 tablespoons chopped **pimiento.**

Crunchy Sesame Seed Dressing

¼	cup finely chopped green pepper
¼	cup finely diced pared cucumber
2	tablespoons minced onion
1	cup thick sour cream
½	cup mayonnaise
1	tablespoon tarragon vinegar
1	tablespoon sugar
1	teaspoon salt
	Few grains pepper
1	clove garlic, crushed in a garlic press or minced
1	tablespoon butter
½	cup sesame seeds
¼	cup (1 oz.) grated Parmesan cheese

1. For Dressing—Mix together green pepper, cucumber, and onion.
2. Drain, if necessary. Mix together sour cream, mayonnaise, tarragon vinegar, sugar, salt, pepper and garlic.
3. Add to vegetables and mix well. Chill thoroughly in refrigerator.
4. For Sesame Seed Topping—While dressing chills, heat butter in a skillet.
5. Add sesame seeds and heat over medium heat until delicately browned, stirring constantly.
6. Remove from heat and add Parmesan cheese.
7. Toss until well blended. Cool.
8. Serve the chilled dressing with cooked or raw **vegetable salads,** or with **mixed greens** or **seafood salads.** Sprinkle the seed topping generously over the dressing.

About 2 cups dressing

Cottage-Blue Cheese Dressing

3	oz. Blue cheese (about ¾ cup, crumbled)
½	cup cream-style cottage cheese
¾	cup thick sour cream
4	teaspoons grated onion
1	tablespoon coarsely chopped pimiento
½	teaspoon salt
½	teaspoon Worcestershire sauce
1	or 2 drops Tabasco

1. Crumble Blue cheese into a bowl.
2. Blend in cottage cheese.
3. Add and blend thoroughly sour cream onion, pimiento, Worcestershire sauce and Tabasco.
4. Store in covered container in refrigerator.
5. If desired, thin with cream before using.

About 1½ cups dressing

Yogurt Salad Dressing

¾	**cup yogurt**
2	**tablespoons mayonnaise**
2	**tablespoons brown sugar**
4	**teaspoons ketchup**
½	**teaspoon salt**

1. Blend together yogurt, mayonnaise, brown sugar, ketchup and salt.
2. Chill thoroughly.

About 1 cup dressing

Piquant Yogurt Salad Dressing: Follow recipe for Yogurt Salad Dressing. Omit ketchup. Decrease brown sugar to 1 tablespoon. Mix in ½ cup **chili sauce,** 2 tablespoons minced **onion,** and 2 tablespoons minced **green pepper.**

Yogurt Fruit Salad Dressing: Follow recipe for Yogurt Salad Dressing. Omit ketchup. Blend in 4 teaspoons **lemon juice.**

Crunchy Yogurt Dressing: Follow recipe for Yogurt Salad Dressing. Mix in ¼ cup chopped toasted blanched **almonds.**

Cheddar Cheese Dressing

4 oz. sharp Cheddar cheese (about 1 cup, grated)
1 cup thick sour cream
1 tablespoon minced parsley
1 tablespoon prepared mustard
1 tablespoon grated onion
½ teaspoon lemon juice
½ teaspoon salt
½ teaspoon Worcestershire sauce
⅛ teaspoon pepper

1. Grate Cheddar cheese.
2. Blend in sour cream.
3. Mix in parsley, prepared mustard, onion, lemon juice, salt, Worcestershire sauce and pepper.
4. Store in covered container in refrigerator.
5. If desired, thin with cream before using.

About 1½ cups dressing

Bacon-Cheese Dressing: Follow recipe for Cheddar Cheese Dressing. Omit lemon juice. Mix in ½ cup crumbled panbroiled **bacon.**

Roquefort-Cheddar Cheese Dressing: Follow recipe for Cheddar Cheese Dressing. Omit prepared mustard. Mix in ¼ cup (about 1 oz.) crumbled **Roquefort cheese.**

Garlic-Cheese Dressing: Follow recipe for Roquefort-Cheddar Cheese Dressing. Omit grated onion. Blend in ½ clove **garlic** crushed in garlic press or minced.

Index

Salad Dressings: